A VICTIM NO MORE

A VICTIM NO MORE

How to STOP Being Taken Advantage Of

LORI REKOWSKI with TIM MIEJAN

Copyright © 2004, 2006, 2012
by Lori Rekowski, AVNM, LLC, with Tim Miejan
All rights reserved, including the right to reproduce this
work in any form whatsoever, without permission
in writing from the publisher, except for brief passages
in connection with a review.

Internet addresses given in this book were accurate at the time it went to press.
Author Lori Rekowski is available as a speaker and consultant.
Please visit www.AVictimNoMore.com for her schedule of appearances.

Cover design by Frame25 Productions
Cover art © Shutterstock.com. All rights reserved.

Library of Congress Cataloging-in-Publication Data

Rekowski, Lori, 1962-
  A victim no more : how to break free from self-judgment / Lori Rekowski
with Tim Miejan.
       p. cm.
  Originally published: Radient Heart Press : Madison, WI, 2004.
  Summary: "Recounts Rekowski's recovery from sexual assault, bulimia, and
depression. Reveals how an underlying 'victim consciousness' in both the victim and the
perpetrator can lead to a vicious cycle of abuse. Shows how she has turned her life
around and offers understanding, encouragement, and meditations to help others do the
same"--Provided by publisher.
  Includes bibliographical references.

  ISBN 978-1-477539-37-8 (5 1/2 x 8 1/2 tp : alk. paper)
  1. Victims of crimes--Psychology. 2. Victims of crimes--Rehabilitation.
3. Victims--Psychology. 4. Self-help techniques. I. Miejan, Tim. II.
Title.
  HV6250.25.R45 2006
  362.88092--dc22
                          2006000330

                    ISBN 978-1-477539-37-8

                       10 9 8 7 6 5 4 3 2

Dedication

When you get lost in the dream...

...You forget that you are the dreamer.

I dedicate this book to all you dreamers who know deep down inside yourselves that you deserve a life filled with peace and contentment—a life filled with joy and bliss.

Contents

A Personal Note from the Author ix

Acknowledgments xv

Foreword, by Wes Hamilton xvii

Introduction xix

1. My Story 1
2. Our Four Major Life Challenges 33
3. Returning to Logic 62
4. Discovering "New Thought" 73
5. Angels among Us 84
6. Helpful Breathing Exercises 88
7. The Healing Power of Music, Dance, and Exercise 94
8. Being Present 99
9. Leaving Fear Behind 103
10. Learning to Create Your New Life 105
11. Getting Real 108
12. What's REALLY in It for You? 120

13. Insights and Exercises 129
14. Support Is Available 158
Recommended Reading and Resources 163

A Personal Note from the Author

This is a book about how I was able to stop being taken advantage of, a book about taking charge of my own life. In some ways, it's a love story. It is a book that offers you ideas, concepts, and resources to draw upon. This isn't a book about some magical date in the future when you will be instantly swept off to heaven, either. It is a book about what you can do *right here, right now*, today, to create your own heaven on this earth. That may feel like a hard pill to swallow if you are in the thick of living your life as a victim, but believe me, it is possible. When you finish the last page of this book, you will have been introduced to all the wisdom and knowledge that you need to lead a healthy and happy life. But it will be up to you to make it happen. You can do it!

1. First, you'll become aware of who you really are. There is a lot of personal power through awareness!

2. Next, you'll learn to fall madly in love with that person. I honestly never thought that I'd be able to, but I can tell you from firsthand experience that it is one incredible feeling!

3. And, last but not least, you will learn how to create a brand-new life that no longer incorporates the word "victim"!

Are you looking for the answers to the age-old questions of: Who am I? What am I doing here? Why do I feel like such a victim in my life? Well, then you've come to the right place. I have answers for those questions and resources to share in this book that I sincerely believe will (among many other great concepts) guide you back into an awareness, and an understanding, that you are a powerful spiritual being having a human experience; a dreamer living in a dream. It is my passion and desire to help you wake up from the dream of living your life in the victim consciousness and turn it into a life that is filled with peace, balance, contentment, and joy. A life that comes from giving to and of yourself, and doing so from a genuine place of self-love. You'll soon discover what a strong and courageous soul you already are while visiting this place called planet Earth: this place where you agreed to come and learn, to evolve, to help others do the same along the way, and, most of all, to become the victor!

To me, to be able to teach you about facing your fears and re-creating the outdated understanding of who you *think* you are is the most important task of this book. Quoting Eleanor Roosevelt: "You gain strength, courage, and confidence by every experience in which you really stop to look fear in the face. You must do the thing which you think you cannot do." And, yes, I did say, who you *think* you are! If you've picked up this book, you've most likely identified with the word "victim." I would venture to say that you have also done so because, like me, you would prefer to believe that you are a "victor" in your life—*not the victim!* I most certainly believe that you can become the champion of your own life, the victor.

Now, finding people that treat you with dignity, compassion, and respect is vital when recovering from traumatic experiences in your life and you have all of that from me. Why? Because once

A Personal Note from the Author

I found the beautiful inner connection to life that was always deep within me, the connection to self-love and self-worth, I've learned to treat *myself* with dignity, compassion, and respect. As a result, I am able to offer that to you from a place of confidence. I know fully that you are a soul who is on the precipice of waking up to the wonderful human being that you came here to be, and I have learned to let go of judging people for whatever circumstances may have led them to where they are today.

Please know that as I share my experiences and triumphs in this book, I do so with a deep compassion and very real understanding of the pain that living in the victim consciousness brings with it. Don't think for a minute that I've forgotten what it was like. I may have learned to forgive, but I most certainly haven't forgotten.

And so, I thank you for letting me be your guide and your teacher in the pages to come.

Lori Rekowski

Please pause now and take a moment to reflect on Richard Bach's wisdom, before we move on.

> Learning is finding out what you already know.
> Doing is demonstrating that you already know it.
> Teaching is reminding others
> That they know just as well as you.
> You are all learners, doers, teachers.
> —*Richard Bach,* Messiah's Handbook

Acknowledgments

Many more people have assisted me on this path than I could ever possibly mention and personally thank here. I must, however, share my deep appreciation for my children, Thomas, Robert, and Lindsey, as they have been the most remarkable and resilient inspirations a parent could dream of having. Thomas, your challenges inspired me to keep pushing myself to learn and grow. Robert, your displays of unconditional love, protection, and acceptance encouraged me, and Lindsey, your unending patience and belief in me humble me. For the three of you to have agreed to participate in such a special plan took great courage. The combination of your patience and endurance in the awakening of my soul took on the form of grace and acceptance that only true angels could offer. I dedicate this book to you, for accepting your roles in this process of releasing the victim consciousness on behalf of so many souls.

I simply cannot miss this opportunity to personally thank Mr. James Redfield for bringing forth the messages of enlightenment through his book *The Celestine Prophecy*. Your work had a great impact on my life, and it has served to awaken so many "light bringers." Yes, with your assistance, we heard the call, James.

The others all know who they are. Amy Mattila, Patricia Hannon, Ellen Sowka, Rustianna Mechura, Kathleen McDowell, Russell Hayden, Alex Cheetham, John Thompson, Wes

Hamilton, Andreas Moritz, and Annee Solis; you've all taught me that I can "grow" beautiful friendships. We are truly "family."

Tim Miejan, how honored I am to have you as my coauthor, and thank you for assisting me to balance and ground the energy of this work. Robert Friedman, I thank you also, for believing in this message and publishing this book, not to mention adding your wisdom and incredible talent to editing it.

And, of course, no words could possibly express the gratitude that I have for those many remarkable ones who provided me with personal, firsthand experiences and lessons, both consciously and unconsciously. I appreciate your support from deep within my soul.

And lastly, I am eternally grateful for those of you who have had the courage to participate in sharing your own insights and challenges, for those of you who have so bravely taken the opportunity to further awaken our souls through your books and articles of wisdom, and for those artists who have painted our visions. Truly, in sharing your glimmerings and guidance for all who would listen, together you have accomplished your mission beautifully.

Foreword

The time for this book has arrived. Having overcome the experience of being a victim for most of her life, Lori Rekowski has emerged a healthy, fully functioning, alive person. In reading this book, I discovered that even though I thought I knew Lori, I realized that she had a secret she was carrying while she was living her life.

We all become victims at one time or another in our lives. Usually, we choose not to share this information with others because of the shame surrounding the experience. This book shines light on the energy of being a victim. It provides validation that being emotionally crippled by being victimized is a normal reaction. Lori shows all of us that we are never alone, that we can ask for help through prayer and friends, and that it can work to move us out of the darkness into the light.

Using the information of an ancient tool, numerology, we can look back on the past century to see that that period was designated as a time for us all to experience the feeling of being victimized. Healing from this experience is helping all of us raise the level of our consciousness. Lori's process is something we can use to walk out of the darkness of feeling alone and into the light of support through affirmations, prayer, and the support of those who really do love us!

—*Wes Hamilton, a friend who loves and supports Lori's quest for love and joy in her life*

Wes Hamilton, president of Insights Consulting and Training, is a national trainer/teacher in the areas of personal and corporate human resource development. With 25 years of experience as a licensed real estate broker in the state of Minnesota, Wes is an expert in the challenges of integrating the body, mind, and spirit as a balance in business. Visit www.weshamilton.com.

Introduction

People are like stained-glass windows.
They sparkle and shine when the sun is out,
but when the darkness sets in,
their true beauty is revealed only
if there is light from within.

—Elisabeth Kübler-Ross

I am about to share some statistics that are a bit mind-boggling to many, and most certainly pertinent to the message that is being shared in this book. Having personally been a victim of—among other personal traumas and crimes in my life—a violent date rape, domestic abuse (on more than one occasion), suicide attempts, and suffering through the murder of a special cousin violently killed while he was helping a neighbor in need, I felt it important for the readers, by viewing how common victimhood really is, to understand the seriousness of the topics in this book. When I say victim consciousness is prevalent in our society, statistics like those listed here back up that statement. By sharing these statistics, I want you to understand clearly that you are obviously not alone in your struggle to shed victim consciousness. We all need to be aware of the true state of our society. Rather than hitting rock bottom in the cycle of misery that is a part of living as a victim, we can become aware that we no longer need to make choices that place us in the path of the victimizers out there in this world. And these statistics prove that there are a lot of them out there.

I once had a police officer tell me that if you place a victim in a room of a thousand people, the victimizer will find that victim, hands down. If you are aware that you are putting off the energy of a victim, you can learn to change that energy and no longer project that vulnerable image out into this world. In recent years, scientists have been able to identify an electromagnetic field around the human heart that is 5,000 times more powerful than the human mind. Other people can feel it five to ten feet away from you. If your heart energy (LOVE) is open, you are radiating positive strong vibrations. That draws positive energy back to you. Like attracts like. Now, if it is closed through fear, people can detect that negative vulnerable energy.

Being aware of the fact that you need to make changes to these energy and behavioral patterns is necessary and part of your first step in healing. Making a commitment to change your life and then sticking with it are the next steps in making the difference in your own life and for our society as a whole. The fewer people who are willing to live their lives as victims, the lower the statistics will fall.

> **Every person, all the events of your life,**
> **are there because you have drawn them there.**
> **What you choose to do with them is up to you.**
> —*Richard Bach,* **Messiah's Handbook**

Once Upon a Choice

Understand that you are *choosing* to make a change in your life, simply by picking up this book and beginning the process of your healing. You are taking action. I applaud you. I realize that life's challenges don't stop and that life continues with all of its personal issues and trials to deal with. We don't have control over the lessons that life offers, such as death, disease, natural disasters, or war. But my goal here is to teach you to hop off the daily drama treadmill, to *not* let others hook you into being pulled into an endless cycle of creating those personal dramas and unpleasant experiences. I'll offer methods that you can apply to your life so that you can begin making new choices to create a brighter future for yourself. Your heart will learn to stay open and radiate much higher vibrations, and that is the kind of energy that you will begin to attract into your own life.

For the Children

I must admit that one of the strongest reasons I had for wanting to get healthy was to be a better mother to my children. And I believe that it is time our children had the opportunity to learn a more compassionate and loving way to live their lives. That begins with you and me being examples of how it can be done. As disturbing as it may be, I'd like you to take a moment and think about how the children represented in the following statistics were affected by the tragedies.

- In 2001, almost 21,000 homicides and 31,000 suicides occurred; and almost 1.8 million people were assaulted, while about 323,000 harmed themselves and were treated in hospital emergency departments. (Surveillance for Fatal and Nonfatal Injuries, 2001, Centers for Disease Control and Prevention National Vital Statistics System)

- Worldwide, an estimated 1.6 million people lost their lives to violence in 2000. About half were suicides, one-third were homicides, and one-fifth were casualties of armed conflict. ("World Report on Violence and Health," World Health Organization, 2002)

- Homicide was the second leading cause of death for people aged 10 to 24 in 2001. Suicide was the third leading cause of death for people aged 10 to 24 in 2002. (Web-based Injury Statistics Query and Reporting System, 2002, Centers for Disease Control and Prevention)

- A recent World Health Organization report estimated the cost of interpersonal violence in the United States (excluding war-related costs) at $300 billion a year. ("The Economic Dimensions of Interpersonal Violence," World Health Organization, 2004)

- The health-related costs of rape, physical assault, stalking, and homicide committed by intimate partners exceed $5.8 billion each year. Of that amount, nearly $4.1 billion are for direct medical and mental healthcare services, and nearly $1.8 billion are for the indirect costs of lost productivity or wages. (Centers for Disease Control and Prevention, Costs of Intimate Partner Violence against Women in the United States, April 2003)

- Seventeen percent of high school girls have been abused physically; 12 percent of high school girls have been abused sexually. ("The Formative Years: Pathways to Substance Abuse among Girls and Young Women Ages 8–22," The National Center on Addiction and Substance Abuse at Columbia University, 2003)

- Of children in sixth through tenth grade, more than 3.2 million—nearly one in six—are victims of bullying each year, while 3.7 million bully other children. ("Bullying Prevention Is Crime Prevention," *Fight Crime: Invest in Kids*, 2003)

- Nearly 60 percent of boys whom researchers classified as bullies in grades six through nine were convicted of at least one crime by the age of 24. Even more dramatic, 40 percent of them had three or more convictions by age 24. ("Bullying Prevention Is Crime Prevention," *Fight Crime: Invest in Kids*, 2003)

- Domestic violence is the single greatest cause of inj women. *(Journal of the American Medical Association)*

- Twenty-two percent of women in the United States have reported being physically assaulted by an intimate partner. (Johns Hopkins University School of Public Health, 1999 [Population Reports, Series L, No. 11])

- In the year 2001, more than half a million American women (588,490 women) were victims of nonfatal violence committed by an intimate partner. (Bureau of Justice Statistics Crime Data Brief, Intimate Partner Violence, 1993–2001, February 2003)

- In 2001, 41,740 women were victims of rape/sexual assault committed by an intimate partner. (Bureau of Justice Statistics Crime Data Brief, Intimate Partner Violence, 1993–2001, February 2003)

- As many as 324,000 women each year experience intimate partner violence during their pregnancy. (J. A. Gazmararian, R. Petersen, A. M. Spitz, M. M. Goodwin, L. E. Saltzman, J. S. Marks. "Violence and reproductive health, current knowledge and future research directions," *Maternal and Child Health Journal 2000,* 4[2]:79–84)

- Thirty-seven percent of women treated in emergency rooms for violent injuries were hurt by a current or former partner. ("Violence Related Injuries Treated in Hospitals," U.S. Department of Justice, August 1997)

- Forty-four percent of women murdered by an intimate partner visited an emergency room in the two years prior to their deaths. ("Predicting Future among Women in Abusive Relationships," *The Journal of Trauma Injury, Infection, and Critical Care,* 2004)

> Experience is not what happens to a man, it is what a man does with what happens to him.
>
> —*Aldous Huxley*

Terms

Many years ago, after attending a workshop in which the topic of judgment came up, I asked my son a simple question: "What would this world be like if there were no judgment?"

He pondered the question for a few moments, looked up into my eyes, and answered with a sweetness and sincerity found in children, "Why, Mom, it would be like heaven."

A Victim No More: How to Break Free from Self-Judgment teaches many tools and principles that you can apply to change your life forever. As I share my story, it will help you move from living as a victim to living free of the old patterns that cause so much pain, frustration, and confusion. An important step in this transformation is to understand the cycle of judgment—of judging yourself and others and situations—and how it can be ended. This book is filled with examples of how releasing judgment allowed me to heal from victimhood by leaps and bounds.

There are a few terms that I use in this book and, with the help of some other authors, I will define them right up front, so as to make your reading experience more enjoyable.

I often team the words "victim" and "consciousness." I use the word "consciousness" in a spiritual sense. Author Patricia Aburdene defined it brilliantly in *Megatrends 2010: The Rise of Conscious Capitalism* (Hampton Roads, 2005) as meaning "presence or alertness—the awareness of awareness, the willingness to observe without attachment, the gleam of Spirit that animates humanity." *Webster's Dictionary* defines "conscious" as "perceiving, apprehending, or noticing with a degree of controlled thought or observation," and "consciousness" as "the quality or state of being aware, especially of something within oneself."

You also may have guessed by now that this is a *spiritual* book. I'd like

Introduction

to define very clearly what I mean by "spiritual" or "spirituality." To do so, I will quote another author, Sharon Janis. Janis wrote an excellent book on the topic of spirituality, titled *Spirituality for Dummies* (IDG Books Worldwide, 2000), which I find full of great insights and wisdom. The book dispels myths about spirituality, one of which states, "*Spirituality is not the same as religion.* Religion is the shell, while spirituality is the kernel within that shell. Religion is the map; spirituality is the territory. Religion is the train; spirituality, the destination." The book also makes it clear that one of the most important aspects of spirituality is to see things from a broader, more long-term perspective.

For me, as I've grown in my own spirituality, my ability to observe my life from a broader perspective has given me the freedom to make more educated and sensible decisions in my life, which has stopped the painful personal dramas that kept me so lost in victim consciousness in the past.

Once again, I'll quote *Webster's Dictionary* here and share its definition of "spirituality" as "the quality or state of being spiritual." And "spiritual" as "relating to, consisting of, or affecting the spirit." Finally, it defines "spirit" as "an animating or vital principle held to give life to physical organisms."

There is increasing awareness in the United States about differentiating spirituality from religion, as this quote from D. Patrick Miller in *A Fearless Bulletin* (July 2005) points out:

> It may surprise many Americans to learn that the number of Christians in our country is steadily declining and that evangelical Christians in particular represent only 7% of the populace, with no increase in their numbers over the last decade. Meanwhile, a full third of American adults now say they are "spiritual but not religious."
>
> Journalists have largely missed the story of America's turn in recent decades toward a deeply felt, personal spirituality that is pursued independently of religious customs and institutions. . . .

In January 2002, a USA TODAY/Gallup poll showed that almost half of American adults do not consider themselves religious. In 1999, 54% said they considered themselves religious; that number had shrunk to 50% in 2002. A full third (33%) described themselves as "spiritual but not religious," an increase of 3% over three years. Ten percent said they regarded themselves as neither spiritual nor religious . . .

According to an American Religious Identification Survey conducted by the Graduate Center of the City University of New York in 2001, the most dramatic demographic shift in religious identification is the number of Americans saying they do not follow any organized religion, increasing from 8% (about 14.3 million people) in 1990 to 14.1% (29.4 million) in 2001.

The last term that I wish to define here is "light worker." Like many other spiritual teachers, I use "love" and "light" interchangeably, as one and the same. I do this from personal and practical experience. As I've healed and evolved spiritually, I've found that I've become lighter (and happier with my life experiences). What I mean by "lighter" is that the more I let go of old resentments, judgments, emotional baggage, destructive habits, and unhealthy patterns which were making my life so miserable, the lighter and more loving toward myself and others I became. My energy level and outlook are and *feel* lighter and brighter each day. Another simple way for me to explain this term is by the following example.

Have you ever walked into a room where people have just been arguing and felt the tension so heavy that you could "cut it with a knife"? It was the *energy* of anger and low-vibration emotions that created that uncomfortable feeling or *energy level*. Greed, hatred, and jealousy are other low-vibration emotions.

How about a time when you attended a celebration, such as a birthday party, wedding, graduation, or holiday festival? Couldn't you just feel your spirits or emotions *rise* to the occasion? Those are higher-frequency or -vibration emotions you were experiencing, such as the loving feelings of joy, happiness, and even bliss. It felt lighter and brighter. As for the second half of the term "light worker," in order to grow, evolve, and transform into a happier and healthier person, one must be persistent and *work* at it. It's as simple as that. But, oh, how that work becomes worth it as you shed your victim consciousness! Years ago when I was a young entrepreneur, a business associate gave me the following quote by Calvin Coolidge. As soon as I read it, I printed it out. Something deep inside me *believed it* and, to this day, I keep it posted on a wall where I can see it daily. It actually became a spiritual "practice" of staying aware (conscious) of the gift that I had deep inside me, a part of my personality makeup, if I may—my natural ability to apply persistence in many areas of my life. I was grateful for that ability.

Persistence

**Nothing in the world
can take the place of persistence.**

**Talent will not;
nothing is more common than
unsuccessful men with talent.**

**Genius will not;
Unrewarded genius is almost a proverb.**

**Education will not;
The world is full of educated derelicts.**

**Persistence and Determination
alone are omnipotent.**

—Calvin Coolidge

My wish for you here is that you too will apply persistence to the *work* on your journey out of victimhood. In using the tools that I will share with you in the pages to come, understand that you can also develop persistence. You can do so by:

- **Understanding your purpose clearly** (no more victimhood!). Keep that burning desire going to support that purpose.

- **Making a commitment followed by a definite plan of action,** including applying a determination to practice the tools that you learn here. Focus on that commitment. Make up some signs with the "author's insights" on them and put them up around your house where you'll see them. Be your own cheerleader or coach and practice, practice, practice those tools.

- **Saying "no" to old negative thoughts** whether from yourself or others who may not want you to change. Just say *no* to those old ways of thinking!

- **Catching yourself immediately** when you start talking negatively or are getting down on yourself. You can do it!

- **Surrounding yourself with others** who want you to succeed and will learn right along with you.

In various parts of the book, I include descriptions of other terms I use, but you will see that if you understand right from the "get-go" the aforementioned terms—consciousness, spirituality, and light worker—as related to my personal teachings here, the journey to healing your victim consciousness will be made a little easier for you.

A Limited View of Our World

Now, many of us who have emerged from living in victim consciousness know all too well that we had been living from a limited view of our world. In the past, we seemed to have gotten stuck in a place where our old habitual thoughts and patterns were all that we knew or could see. These habitual thoughts and patterns felt familiar to us. They also limited us. All too often, our decisions had been made from an automatic response or reflex, rather than from being able to step back and observe it all from our full human potential. The automatic response came not only from the beliefs that we adopted as children as coping skills, but from beliefs that we held about our life based on our past experiences. These beliefs, whether positive or negative, created the person that we became as an adult. Some of our beliefs were easy to identify, especially our negative ones, such as: "I am a failure" or "I am too tall, too thin, too fat, not smart enough," etc. Others were invisible and we didn't even know we had them. Once we release the past and the old beliefs that were holding us back, we can leave victimhood behind, and our body, mind, and soul can work in harmony to create a balanced, happy life. We now will learn to develop the ability to see the "big picture" and hold an expanded viewpoint, so that the emptiness and loneliness that accompanied victimhood will become mere memories.

Our life can be free of the confusion, pain, suffering, and traumas we have experienced in the past as incomplete human beings. By stepping out of self-judgment and into self-acceptance, we can move into a place of amazing beauty and serenity together and use this broader view of our world to heal others and ourselves. Changing or transforming a pattern, habit, or belief is the essence of healing, and exploring new insights and practices will begin the process for you. You will discover that you may have been holding on to beliefs that no longer serve you. You can learn to observe yourself and the old ways in which you dealt with life, and then get your chi energy (life energy) flowing according to your new, more positive mindset. You can also discover how to pull out of the cobwebs some of the more positive beliefs that you had as a child (before others squashed them) and follow some of those dreams, if you so choose. Once on this journey of true self-discovery and living a joy-filled life, you may just discover that you have more choices than you ever dreamed possible.

Being a Victim

Living from a victim mindset is more common than one might think or care to admit. Being a victim can be explained as "giving one's power away to someone or something else." That "something else" can be a situation, an event, whatever happens to you that makes you feel less worthy or as if you had been treated unfairly. When we're perfectly honest, each of us has adopted a "poor me" attitude at one point or another.

Blame and guilt are common reactions we all have used to deal with something we felt was unfair. Stop, look around, and truly observe our society for a moment. It does not take long to see that this consciousness and attitude permeate our culture. Is there really one of you who hasn't felt you have gotten a raw deal, or had a family member or friend who hasn't expressed this attitude at one time or another? Each of us knows plenty of people who live their lives complaining out loud, daily, about getting a raw deal. After a while, that complaining becomes bitterness and anger.

Whether it's a feeling of being overwhelmed by new parenthood with all of its new demands; or a feeling of resentment for having to care for your aging parents; or dealing with the aging process yourself; or having a child dealing with addictions; or worrying about your son or daughter in the military, at war halfway around the world; or going through a catastrophic event such as losing your home in a flood, hurricane, earthquake, or other act of Mother Nature; or remembering what it was like to be teased or bullied as a child in school—you can relate to this book. Maybe you've experienced infidelity in your marriage, or the exasperation of dealing with a virus or other illness. Maybe you've been overlooked for a promotion at work. Victimhood is something we all experience. We have all been there at one time or another. We have all felt like a victim. We have all said "poor me."

Introduction

Some may associate victimhood with people who are experiencing a drama-filled lifestyle, perhaps with one failed relationship after another, frequent job changes, or even rape, child abuse, or spousal abuse. Understand that no matter whether we "label" or think of ourselves as victims or not, the consciousness of victimhood has thoroughly penetrated our actions or reactions through indoctrination by our society as a whole. Our feelings of powerlessness, of not feeling or being in control in various situations in our lives, bring up all sorts of uncomfortable and ugly emotions in each of us and, in turn, those around us respond accordingly. They mirror our actions and emotions right back to us and we draw more of the same negative experiences. And so the cycle continues and compounds itself until we often feel out of control.

What we have forgotten along the way is that each of us does have control at any point in time. We can choose to control our attitudes and responses in every single situation! Many people prefer, however, to give their control or beliefs over to others in their everyday lives, just as many want that control over others. We can begin to change that pattern right here, right now, by choosing to learn new ways of interacting with others and ourselves.

In this book, I will share with you insights—and offer you tools—on how you can choose new ways of viewing life, and acting rather than reacting. Applying these tools will change your life for the better. You will stay empowered and find your inner peace, no matter what life brings your way.

The more you understand that you can take responsibility for your life without the indoctrination of guilt and shame, and the more you learn how to choose to react from a loving, respectful, and self-honoring way, from that place of integrity within, the more you will understand how you, too, can live a more harmonious, peaceful, fulfilling, love-filled, and balanced lifestyle. Absorb and practice the tools on the pages to come and you will begin to trust in your own abilities far more than you ever dreamed possible. Remember, what you focus your thoughts on today is creating the vibrations that make up your future experiences. Furthermore, you can say "enough is enough," and leave that old, negative way of thinking behind!

When you catch yourself falling back into negative thought patterns from the past, change those thoughts, right at that moment, and redirect them to something that reminds you of joy and happiness in your life. It could be a memory of your first love, of holding your child in your arms for the first time, of winning a contest, or simply of a delightful summer day playing in the water at a beach. Thinking of anything happy and joyful will work. Focusing on your past—and the old victim way of thinking—only creates more of what you had. Changing your thoughts to something more positive will move your life toward what you dream it can be.

A brief note: I was raised in the Christian faith, so as you read this book, understand that some of my interpretations are, to a degree, reflective of that indoctrination. In applying the "Golden Rule" to my life, I honor the people of all religions. I cherish the unity that is now spreading across this planet through so many organizations, such as the Center for Nonviolent Communication (www.cnvc.org) and many others that can be found on the Internet (see www.be-progressive.us/peace-linx.html). These groups are striving to remove the "right and wrong" mindset that for centuries has caused wars on our planet. To end violence, they are working hard to replace such strife with peace and acceptance of one another's personal beliefs. My hope is that by sharing in and experiencing that transformation together, healing that old consciousness—that source of victim consciousness—we can boot it right out of the consciousness of humanity today!

The Word "Victim" Isn't Just about Women Anymore

I also want to make it clear that this book is not just for women. Through the process of writing this book, I came to the realization that even though I often found myself overpowered by the physical strength of men, I also choose to give equal credit to those male "angels" who played out the roles of rescuer and compassionate helper in my life.

As you will discover, men have helped me escape victimhood, and I have been of assistance to many men as a result. I would also like to share here that my dear brother-in-law, Peter, who left our physical plane in August 2003, assisted me in sorting out and processing my ideas while I wrote the first draft of this book. I am eternally grateful to him. My sister, in tribute to Peter, designed a special thank-you note to acknowledge the friends, family, and neighbors who sent sympathy cards and helped with the funeral arrangements, as well as the generosity of those who brought gifts of food to the family following his passing. Quoting John Lennon's "Instant Karma," she wrote: "We all shine on, like the stars, the moon, and the sun." Peter's energy does shine through in this book—and always will.

Some of my greatest cheerleaders in getting this book out to the public have been, and still are, male friends. In reflection, many of the men who most influenced me on my life's path were those who kept me moving toward the light of shedding the victim consciousness. It is my desire that the teachings in this book also assist the many men out there who are caught in victim consciousness in getting on their path to healing. It is vital that we honor the gender reality, for the time has come to balance the energy of our female and male aspects of self and to celebrate the healing together. There are no gender specifics or differences when it comes to experiencing victimhood or victim consciousness. Although our society's perception may lead us to believe that men are not victims, we all know that this is not the truth.

Over the years, I have practiced the art of "letting go and letting God" and participate daily in healing our planet, one person at a time, starting with me. I take responsibility, joyously, in my work now, and I am not worried about changing the world anymore. The Creator can handle that in Its Unity. And by that I mean all of us working together! That can mean you, me, our angels and guides, and all living beings together as one.

I do my best to stay in gratitude, even when I do not especially feel like it or understand why I should. That is important. Gratitude is one powerful tool! And choosing gratitude can be a simple choice. Practice it a bit every day so it soon becomes a habit. I'm the first to admit there have been times when I've lain on the bed sobbing and actually said, "Thank you, anyway . . . I don't know why I am going through this and, frankly, it's awful at the moment, but I do know that it's for the highest good of all!"

Fortunately, we are in a time of releasing the want, need, or desire for suffering. Cheers to that new reality!

I have also found that when you focus on changing yourself, you become part of the process as a whole. What joy! Personal awareness brings with it power—the power to change and grow.

A Reminder of My Own Spiritual Path

Once, on a train ride back to Minnesota from Washington State in the mid-1970s, I met a woman who shared with me that she thought we are all "lights" or "energies," and that a part of us, or that light, remains with others when we leave them. That felt so right and made sense to me. She did not tell me that what I believed was wrong. She didn't tell me what to believe at all. She simply shared with me what she believed. At the time, I had never heard of such a thing, but the concept resonated with me like nothing else I'd heard before. I have thought of that conversation many times in the years since then. By the time I was 16, I had begun to contemplate the confusing nature of religion. My friends who were Catholic were told it was a sin to attend my church, and my Baptist church made it known that the Catholics were "wrong" about many of their beliefs. This "right and wrong" issue did not ring true to me at all. Having talent as a singer, I formed a gospel-singing group comprised of Baptists, Catholics, Methodists, and Lutherans. We sang at all of the different churches and were surprisingly accepted with open arms, even in the conservative city where I grew up in the Midwest.

I guess you could say I've always been a leader in sharing new ideas, a bit "outside the box" in my ways. I do hope that each of you reading this book understands that I am sharing the information here from my heart—with a love that is unlimited and hopeful for humanity. I've made it out of the victim consciousness and I believe that you can, too!

Yes, I have had much more trauma in my life than most people, but I also enjoyed my share of very happy memories from my childhood, such as riding my own horse, Ringo, traveling out West on vacations every year, celebrating holidays, touring with my gospel singing group, going to basketball and football games, snowmobile riding, swimming, and summer Bible camps. As I have healed, I have learned to remember and focus on more positive experiences of my childhood, rather than just on the more painful ones. I also have come to an understanding that my parents did what their parents taught them to, and they did the best they could. Now, in this present moment, we all have a choice to change the cycle; we can choose not to pass a limited mindset on to our children. Instead, we can usher in the new age of higher, more enlightened consciousness, with its bright and exciting new future. How thankful I am to be a part of that change.

I will share some out-of-the-ordinary experiences and miracles with you. In the spirit of positive change, I challenge you to refrain from placing negative judgments on these experiences. They may seem a little different from what you are used to. Then again, they may not. As I have shared some of these experiences in my workshops, I found people to be quite interested and aware of some of these types of experiences—more so than not, actually. And so let us stay grounded and focused as we reflect together. I invite you to use what speaks to you in the pages that follow and, please, just leave the rest for a future time and place. Everything happens in Divine order.

Practice the tools that I share in the pages to come and you will begin to trust in your own abilities to a far greater extent than you ever felt possible. Remember, what you focus your thoughts on today creates the vibrations that will make up your future experiences. Again, you have the power to say, right now, "That's it, enough is enough!" as you leave those old ways of thinking behind. If you catch yourself falling back into negative thoughts or "self-talk" from the past, know that you have the power to change those thoughts, right here, right now.

1
My Story

Angels may not always come when you call them, but they will come when you need them.

—*Karen Goldman*

    Summarizing the first 40 years of living my life in the throes of victim consciousness isn't an easy task. Telling my story takes a concentrated effort to stay positive on my part. It is difficult to summarize the painful memories of my life, but I am doing so here in order to help as many people as possible. I want you, the reader, to understand that you aren't alone in your life struggles, that there are many others who have had similar experiences and came through them as better people. Attempting to write only about the areas of my life that *directly pertain* to portraying the various life challenges that I listed in the introduction wasn't simple to do either. To say that it was a bit of a stretch out of my comfort zone is putting it mildly.

    However, I've chosen to share some of the stories about my struggles with my marriages, weight problems, various addictions, traumas, and issues that millions of people around the world have also gone through. I sensed as the writing process continued and evolved that you may want to have a closer look into some of the patterns and behaviors that I was immersed in while living my life in the victim mindset. I offer these descriptions in hope that you will see that even someone who has had as many years of struggles as I did can come out on the other side, the victor! The only way I felt that I could do this was to open up my life, let my pride go, and get into some of the details of what I went through. Of course, I couldn't go into every detail, but I've highlighted many of the challenges as well as I could and as accurately as possible in the time sequencing.

During this process, I widened my view and looked into the past *as an observer*. I've reminded myself that I am here now, and that the past is just that, the past. It has no hold on me anymore. When I do this, I don't get pulled into the painful emotions of the experiences and I can be more detached as I learn the lesson that those experiences brought me, even as I write them down on paper. In fact, it helps me to pretend that I am watching a movie I starred in rather than making myself go through the dramas as if they are happening all over again. It's a great tool. When I feel myself being pulled into the "movie" and getting uncomfortable, I say to myself, "This is not who I am, this is what I experienced." It really does help me to stay in the now and appreciate how far I've come and also to realize that I *had* that experience; I *wasn't* the experience!

As I tell this story, I do so by giving you glimpses of the "old Lori," the one who lived her life as a victim, and what that personal journey was like. I do this with the intention of sharing what I learned from those experiences and just exactly how far I've come. I truly count my blessings now and appreciate how fortunate I am to be alive. I look back at that "old Lori," the one who was stuck in victim consciousness, and now as part of my healing process, I send her love and compassion as her "future self."

A Very Helpful Exercise to Share

Louise Hay taught a little exercise in her "Heal Your Life" program, which had you imagine your parents (first your father and then your mother) as small children. She had you shrink them down so that you could fit them in your hand and then tell them that everything would be okay, that you love them unconditionally. She then had you pretend to place them within your heart. I just loved that exercise! Remembering that my parents were innocent children who went through their own painful lessons before they became my parents somehow helped me to release judgment on them and embrace them as the spiritual beings that they are. That is when I learned to do the same thing for myself. I would often imagine myself as a little girl or teenager and guide myself back to a memory of one of the traumas that I experienced. I, as her future self, would hug her and tell her that everything was going to be okay. This really was an amazingly powerful exercise, and I could feel the self-love and compassion come through me for the hurt little child that I was. I could feel this experience heal me on many levels. I grow to have more self-love and compassion for myself when I do this. I understand now that this tool (of observing and healing my "past self") is extremely valuable.

I taught this exercise to a new friend once. A few months later, after a breakup with his girlfriend, he was completely devastated. He said that he even was feeling suicidal. He then remembered the exercise and shared with me later that he actually felt as if it saved his life. I tell you this to encourage you to try it out yourself. It really is remarkable to experience that kind of healing for yourself.

Increasing My Ability to Love Myself

Today, in my new victim-free mindset, I am committed to increasing the love for myself in many ways. I work at it daily. Yes, life's painful memories will rise to the surface. But now, even when I am right smack-dab in the middle of vividly remembering and *feeling* the struggles and the pain, I can happily share that I have the capability to heal the inner child within by using the new techniques and exercises that I've learned. The exercise that I just mentioned is one of those tools. I have many more of these tools that I will share in this book to be used on your healing path.

I hold the realization that to put myself down or negatively judge those past behaviors, actions, and experiences (as I used to do regularly) is fruitless. It only defeats my efforts to maintain my inner peace and happiness. What a difference changing that old judgmental pattern has made in my life today!

Breaking free from judging myself was my biggest task by far—and how. It has been a remarkably successful practice toward loving myself wholly. Now, with that in mind, I share . . .

Here It Is, My Story

In my life, there were men who harmed me, and men who came to my rescue. One of those men who came to my rescue was a police officer who literally saved my life the night of my near-death experience in November 1998, not long after my landlord had sexually assaulted me. At the time, I was caught up in the unpleasantness of divorcing my second husband. My nerves were shot as the result of what was taking place in my life. My home-based consulting business was failing. In an attempt to make ends meet, I had taken a job with an airline company, both for the income and to be able to travel for my consulting business, which had been all but halted by the responsibilities and demands of my failed marriage. To save money, my three children and I had moved from a 2,200-square-foot home into a one-bedroom apartment. Within five months of that move, my new landlord sexually assaulted me and, as a result, I emotionally couldn't handle my job and quit. That left me without an income and unable to pay my rent. Needless to say, it was a difficult time in my life, and I felt as though I had failed my children, family, and friends. I was seeking a way to escape, to end it all. I didn't see any other way out of my misery.

Before I proceed, let me share a bit more about my life up to that life-changing event of the near-death experience.

Misery and Confusion

Back then, it was a mystery to me as to why I was here, in this body, in these circumstances. I didn't have a clue about how to identify with myself as a spiritual being having a human experience. I was locked into living in emotional pain a majority of the time. The ups and downs of my mental, physical, and emotional conditions were extremely frustrating to navigate and no matter what I did to seek help, none was to be found. Why did I lack the ability to find the peace that evaded me for so many years? A sense of desperation lingered in my life. I traveled from one addictive behavior to another. I traveled blindly with no comprehension or hint of understanding as to why the darkness had come over me.

Clearly, I had chosen a path of struggle, with one drama after another. I experienced childhood incest and obesity. I became bulimic when I was 17 and then was traumatized by a violent date rape in college. I endured more sexual assaults and years of adolescent depression—depression and despair followed me into my adult years—and I attempted suicide in both childhood and adulthood. I experienced nine years of being stalked by an obsessive person whose identity, to this day, I've yet to know. I "participated" in abusive relationships, went through two divorces, abused alcohol at times, experienced homelessness, struggled with child-custody battles, suffered a miscarriage, had an abortion, and was involved in three auto accidents. I went on to fail in several businesses, suffered in poverty, fractured the base of my spine in a fall, and developed physical illness that required four surgeries in five short months—all of this, I realize today, was out of pure oppression! That oppression was caused by my ignorance of the concept of unconditional love. I had little, if any, comprehension of self-love, self-esteem, or self-respect. The bottom line: Those painful years of suffering were the result of a lack of knowledge and my inability to understand or feel the connection with God that had always been there—within me. The Light was always there; I had simply forgotten.

Had I agreed to a sacred contract before this lifetime that meant I would experience these difficulties so I could assist others in their awakening process? That story continues to unfold. Remember, as a spiritual being, we are never alone—and never were.

Extraordinary Experiences

At the tender age of 12, I suffered from adolescent depression and horrific mood swings. One day, I was having an emotional conversation with my pastor, who, unbeknownst to me, had recently been told by the elders of the church that he should cast demons out of me. (Years later, I learned that this was a practice from the Middle Ages, when mental illnesses came to be viewed as conditions to cure, with demonic possession or witchcraft as their cause.) I suddenly looked him right in the eye and told him frankly, in a matter-of-fact way through my tears, "I am going through all of this horrible pain and will go through much, much more, so I can help thousands of people in the future." As the old saying goes, "Out of the mouths of babes."

Let me also expound a bit here on "demon possession." It's common in the Christian religion to deem negative entities "demons." The 1973 film *The Exorcist* highlighted demonic possession like never before. I was convinced that the pastor and elders must be right, and I continued to experience strange occurrences and outright terror after having been told I was possessed. In fact, a short time after my conversation with the pastor, while living in Washington State for the winter, I decided I must indeed be possessed, for once again, I had had a violent argument with my older sister. I went into my bedroom, lay on the bed, and repeated, over and over and over again: "In the name of Jesus Christ, I command you to leave me." I have always, even as a child, had a "knowing" or "faith" that the light would always win out over the darkness. After repeating that phrase, I experienced what I now understand was an "out-of-body experience" (OBE). Of course, I didn't understand or know that term back then. But there I was, floating above my body and looking right down at it from above. When I returned to my body, I knew that it was over, that I was no longer possessed, and my life actually began to return to a semi-normal state. My grades improved, I made friends more easily, the violent temper left me, and I had a much happier next couple of years.

After that occurrence, I began having the same dream over and over again: A man of dark complexion would point at me and then beckon with his finger, saying, "Come, come, come" in a very disturbing way. The dream sequence was set in the same house that I had lived in at the time of the out-of-body experience. In my dream, every time I tried to get out of the house, he would be at the door or window, staring at me, saying, "Come, come, come . . ." Then the house would burst into flames and I couldn't get out unless I went to him. I always woke up before I died.

When I shared that dream with other kids my age, they began to tell me their own stories about strange things that had happened to them. They talked of books flying around their rooms and doors opening and closing when no one was there. I heard hundreds of poltergeist and ghost stories. Each time they shared their own experiences, they seemed relieved to have someone who understood. Even as a child, I made it my mission to tell them that they didn't have to be afraid anymore, that they too could have the Christ light cast away the dark ones. At times, while I was sharing knowledge with others, couches would rise up off the floor, water would turn on by itself, and other unexplainable circumstances would occur. Those things did not stop me from helping others, for I had become fearless in my desire to teach others how to rid themselves of those "scary" entities and situations.

Mysteries would arrive to me at the most unexpected times. I had flashbacks of times and places that I could not possibly have known in this lifetime. They were memories of places far away and so long ago. I had visions and dreams, as well as other odd perceptions that were certainly out of the normal realm of this current time. Later in my life, I read the book *Many Lives, Many Masters*, by Dr. Brian Weiss, which helped me connect the dots. Much to my pleasure (and peace of mind that followed this discovery), the book documented a case that explained these memories and experiences. It revealed clearly to me that I had been spontaneously recalling past-life experiences.

That understanding helped me become aware of how different I was. In a world of rules and regulations that allowed for no such acceptance of these "gifts," I floundered. These gifts were unacceptable at the time of my childhood, and my mysterious and wondrous experiences created more despair in me.

My Turbulent Teenage Years

In my junior and senior high school years, I drifted in and out of intense religious periods, at times disciplining myself into total compliance with my church's views and at other times rebelling. I always ended up feeling like I was living for others when I was in the intense religious periods, but I seemed to please my parents and church leaders when I was doing so. And that had its advantages. Every child wishes to be accepted and I was, most certainly, no different. In hindsight, I now see that the problem was that I knew down deep inside that I wasn't living my own truth, but someone else's. I just couldn't find peace in the doctrine that I was being taught. Living that way doesn't work in the long haul.

At 16, I ran away from home and then attempted suicide once again. The second night into the hospital stay after that attempt, the new minister at my church, whom I had gotten to know quite well, visited me and suggested that I attempt to find a new understanding of God. Yet I wasn't quite sure how to do that. I was sent to a social worker for counseling at my doctor's recommendation, and I really enjoyed working with her. However, it didn't last long when she began to teach me new ways to view my world, and myself. My parents disagreed with her belief systems and what she was teaching me, and they wouldn't allow me to see her anymore. I was sad, angry, and confused about that decision. However, I seemed to have garnered some much-needed wisdom and valuable insights from the time that I spent with her and was able to function much better. By the way, many years later, after bumping into that counselor at a store, I reconnected again for a brief visit. Much to my delight, I found out that she was a light worker. She was an open-minded, spiritual person who had dedicated her life to healing others. Although she hadn't shared her personal spiritual views with me during the time that I went to her for counseling, I discovered through our visit that they were very similar to the way I believe now. I found that to be nothing but synchronicity at work in my life. Even during the 30 intervening years, I was sent teachers who were there to help me remember who I really was.

By my junior year of high school, I weighed 231 pounds. I started a job and, in doing so, I started to feel better about myself. I proceeded to lose 80 pounds in nine months. I had never felt so wonderful in my life. I loved going back to school that fall, as a senior and a new and completely different-looking person. I enjoyed the beginning of that senior year, although after an unpleasant encounter with my group of friends that I mention later in this book, that all changed. After that experience, I developed an eating disorder and spent a period of time in which I basically locked myself in my room every night and read the Bible. I withdrew from many of my school activities and began gaining weight again. *I observe now that I tended to live the "all or nothing lifestyle" and this was the perfect example.*

Off to College

After I graduated from high school, I went to live with my aunt about a half an hour away from my hometown. I worked for my aunt that summer and often stayed with my grandmother and had a chance to really get to know her for the first time. I enjoyed the time that I spent with them both and worked full time at my aunt's A & W. I lost the weight I had gained and headed off to college that fall, but I only made it through my first semester. I loved being out on my own and was running three miles a day, in the best shape of my life, yet I was struggling with bulimia and with handling the stress of a new life out on my own. I was overwhelmed with the change. I fell into partying too often and was dating regularly for the first time in my life. All of these changes were just too much for me emotionally. Having dated rarely during my high school years, having been sexually assaulted as a child, and still suffering from low self-esteem, I wasn't handling it all very well. I lost my virginity that autumn, on a night when I was drunk, and the guy basically blew me off after a couple of dates. I didn't know what to do with the feelings of rejection that came along with that experience. And I wasn't about to discuss it with my mother. She had already told me that if I ever got pregnant, I would basically be disowned. I really knew nothing of how to set proper boundaries and experienced a lot of fear and confusion in navigating the whole dating scene. I was so excited about my social life, though, that, unfortunately, my studies became second to it and my grades suffered. I finished out the semester and then decided to move back home and get a job, with plans and hopes to go back to college the following year. I was disappointed in myself and so were my parents.

Moving to the Big City

Six months later I headed to a suburb of Minneapolis, moving in with my sister, and got a job for the summer. I was suffering from the regret of having dropped out of college in the first place and went into a tailspin with the eating disorder. Living in the big city was a whole different world for me yet again, and although I loved the action and excitement of this new life, I was experiencing a lot of anxiety from all of the changes. I found a treatment program at the University of Minnesota (one of the first for eating disorders in the country) and started feeling much better by the end of it. For the first time in my life, I felt as if someone understood my eating problems and I learned some new ways of dealing with my old habits of turning to food when I was upset. It helped for a while.

Back to College

That fall I gave college another attempt. I registered at the University of Minnesota. While moving into the dormitory, I took my new roommate aside and shared with her that I had just been through an eating disorder program for bulimia. Under the advice of my counselor, I told her about the disease and that I was working on my program. I also asked her if she minded if we didn't get a refrigerator in our room. Much to my dismay, she immediately took me out of the room where her boyfriend was and then confided in me that she too was bulimic and had never told anyone! Well, it didn't take long and I was right back in the old behavior pattern. In fact, I discovered that one of my childhood friends who attended a college nearby also had become bulimic, and the three of us would go out to eat together and head into the bathroom and purge. I discovered firsthand that I really wasn't alone at all in experiencing that disorder and furthermore that there was an epidemic of it in the colleges at that time.

The partying atmosphere and free-for-all binging on food and alcohol were again too much for me to handle emotionally. I was out partying constantly and on New Year's Eve got a DUI ticket. I had just finished up the semester with a major in law enforcement and I discovered that by getting that ticket, it was the end of that dream. I couldn't become a police officer with a DUI on my record. Once again, the drama was building up in my life! I was advised by my boss, who had just been through an alcohol treatment program, to check into a 28-day treatment program and I did so. I had no choice but to drop out of college. My treatment counselor soon recognized that I had bulimia (his wife was bulimic) and came to the conclusion that the eating disorder was my primary "drug of choice." It was all very confusing. I completed the program but was exposed to some of the most horrible victim stories I've ever heard. In fact, I would say that the whole experience of that treatment program left me more traumatized than I was before I went in and did little more than confuse me.

A Church Experience I Won't Forget

After completing the treatment program, I went to work in various jobs and, through one of my roommates, ended up joining a cult-like church for a while. Although it was Christian-based, it had some very strict doctrines and I was told that I really wasn't "saved," as I hadn't been baptized for my salvation. My parents disagreed strongly and the push and pull of the two different belief sets got me even more screwed up! The church people told me that I should stay away from my family altogether. I had a realization about three months into the experience with that church that it wasn't going to work for me when they attempted to get me to live with one of their church members and advised me to disassociate with my old friends as well. I was advised not to be spending time with my other friends and family because they didn't believe the same way, and something deep down inside me told me to get out of that group. Fortunately, I did, but I was heading for an even more difficult situation.

The Date Rape

I had found a roommate through my job. I barely knew her, but I did know that I needed to find a new place to live. I'd been moving around a lot; she seemed like a normal person and she was looking for a roommate, so I agreed to move in. It worked out great at first, but I soon found out that her lifestyle wasn't one that I had been subjected to before; and let's just say that she wanted to include me in her sexual life. I said no, and left it at that. I'm not judgmental about bisexuals, gays, or lesbians. I never was, and even though my church said that they were living in sin, I didn't buy it. It just wasn't a lifestyle that I enjoyed participating in. I did, however, go out to bars with her a few times. On one occasion she suggested that we invite some men to our apartment. I was still very naïve when it came to men, as I'd only dated for a couple of years on and off in college. That night, one of the men violently raped me and, much to my dismay, when I called out to my roommate for help, she just took him into the bedroom with her and the other guy and let him join their party. When I found the man still there the next morning, I was completely confused as to what to do about it. There they were, the three of them acting as if nothing had happened and all was just peachy keen. I moved out within two days. I didn't call the police because we had invited them to our apartment, and so I thought that they wouldn't believe me. It also was just their word against mine, and I was afraid that I would look like a complete liar. I didn't phone my parents either, as I thought for sure that they would make me move home.

Out on My Own and in Love for the First Time

I just blocked the experience out in my mind, stuffed it deep down inside, and decided to pretend that it had never happened. I then moved back in with my sister and I was working full-time once again. Months later, I met a man and fell madly in love for the first time. Within a year, I became pregnant. We were planning the wedding of my dreams when I had the miscarriage. After having an emotional conversation with my fiancé's roommate, who then shared with me that my fiancé had told him that he wanted to wait a while to get married, I decided to postpone the wedding. I found out later that he had not wanted to tell me because he didn't want to hurt me. I was confused and grieving from the miscarriage. To make matters worse, I also had complications from the miscarriage and had to have surgery. My parents were very displeased and I felt terrible guilt about the whole experience. Once again, the eating disorder flared up severely.

The Disappointment

Months later I flew out to the state of Washington from my home in Minnesota to check into an inpatient eating-disorder program. There had been a television report about Pat Boone's daughter having been successfully treated for an eating disorder at this hospital. I had high hopes of finding the help I needed and getting my life back in order. And since I had been binge eating and purging up to *15 times a day*, in desperation I phoned my parents and we made arrangements for me to check in. My fiancé bought me a beautiful bouquet of flowers and sent me off with a feeling of hope for a new beginning.

I adjusted to the program quickly but less than a week into that program, I was told that I wasn't sick enough to be an inpatient! I could hardly believe my ears. I had been throwing up 15 times a day, even while on breaks at work. I was terribly upset, yet with no other choice at hand, I flew back to Minnesota to find out that my first love had decided to end our relationship. I was crushed! He had been the love of my life, my best friend, and we hadn't even had a turbulent relationship at all. In fact, we rarely had arguments. I didn't even see it coming and was shocked.

Another Assault

A few weeks after the breakup, I had fallen asleep on the couch after a night of partying with my friends. I was awakened by a strange man that was—well, let's just say, was molesting my breasts. I was terrified! Along with the shock of waking up to this experience came the realization that I knew that my roommate had been seeing some men who were doing drugs. And, believe me, this man was on drugs that night. I'd never seen the man before. I had been wearing a sundress and he had simply pulled it down and molested me. He stepped back and informed me that he was my roommate's boyfriend and then walked away and into her bedroom when I frantically told him to get away from me.

I had only recently (a month before) moved in with this

woman because one of her other roommates had gone to my church and told me that they had a room available. The gal from church had moved out a few weeks after I moved in, as did another roommate, because this other woman had been abusive to them. I didn't have anywhere else to go at that time, so I stayed. I had already figured out that she wasn't exactly a stable person. I was her sixth roommate in less than six months!

There I was in this frightening situation and I ran into my bedroom and shut the door. I finally had fallen back to sleep when the same awful thing awakened me again. He was in my bedroom molesting me again. This time, I screamed and my roommate came in. To make matters worse, she began blaming me for the situation and insinuated that I'd asked for it. Life was throwing me one nightmare after another and it was just unbelievable. I had started dating this woman's cousin (later to become my husband) and he, too, later insinuated that I had somehow led my roommate's boyfriend on, which shocked me even further. How could they even say that, when I was sound asleep? I felt ashamed and humiliated. I phoned one of the other girls who had lived there and she invited me to move in with her at her new place. The constant moving was really getting to me, even at that age. I still had more traumas to come.

My First Marriage

It was then that I checked into an outpatient program that was just beginning to treat eating disorders (following the hospital's recommendations). I had, for some reason, continued to see the man I was dating, although I was still not over my first love. Rebound and vulnerability are two words that now come to mind with those memories.

He was a recent Catholic convert who had become a born-again Christian and my parents liked that fact. And, frankly, it soothed me as well. His beliefs felt familiar and his devotion to Bible studies and God was comforting to me, as I was feeling very vulnerable and hurt at that time. He was also a recovering alcoholic and very intense. I became pregnant a month after we begin to sleep together and struggled with whether I should marry him or not. I broke up with him for a short time and just couldn't bring myself to have an abortion because of my religious beliefs. I gave in and went back to him and did what my family and he wanted me to do. I put it off until I was five months along but finally decided to marry him. My parents wouldn't let me invite any friends or relatives because of my pregnancy, and it wasn't exactly the happiest day of my life. We had a fairly small wedding, although most of his relatives attended it. I was really very sad not to have my close friends and aunts and uncles in attendance, and I still wasn't sure on that morning if I really wanted to marry him. But I did, and my sister was kind enough to host the reception at her house.

Within the first year into our marriage, although I was delighted to have a beautiful baby boy, I was generally miserable. I had gained a lot of weight during my pregnancy, and my son also was sick. The doctors wouldn't believe me when I told them that he was spitting up almost all of his food after he ate, and it took six months before they did. By then, he had stopped growing and was horribly thin. They placed him in the hospital for a weeklong series of tests and then had to perform major surgery to save his life.

Once again, life was hitting me hard; to make matters worse, the surgeon who operated on my son failed to tell us that he didn't believe in giving pain medication to babies as he felt that they healed faster without it. We were frantically trying to soothe our baby as he cried for the entire next day. The only time he would stop was when we pushed him in his stroller. We put in many miles walking that floor of the hospital! Finally, after he hadn't even been able to sleep, I called the other specialist who had recommended the surgeon and pleaded that he do something. He ordered some sleeping medication and finally my baby was able to get some rest.

Now, during the time that we were at the hospital I was feeling very ill. I thought that it was just the stress and strain of the whole experience, but soon I discovered that I was pregnant with my second child. My son's surgery was successful, and life seemed to settle down for us all for a while. We moved into a new home not long after our second son was born. Only two short weeks into living there, we had a pipe burst while we were out of town and came home to yet another stressful event. Most of our belongings were either ruined or damaged and we had to find a place to live while the pipe was being repaired. The stress of that situation exacerbated my struggling marriage. I just couldn't take it anymore. I separated from my husband and moved with my boys up to my hometown. My parents were not pleased at all. After four months of being separated, my husband convinced me to come back. He had written me letters, called, and promised me that things would be better. I decided to try once more.

Going for Help Once Again

I began to have relapses with the eating disorder not long after the return and was very unhappy with the fact that my husband's promises had been broken once again. In an effort to find some sort of relief, I chose to go back to the University of Minnesota for help. I was put on yet another new and experimental program for treating bulimia. They put me on nearly 300 times the dose of Prozac (an antidepressant drug) that a normal patient being treated for depression would have been prescribed. They told me that it was a new type of treatment for eating disorders and recommended that I try it. That high dosage sent me into a horrible emotional state and when I phoned the emergency room to describe what was happening, the doctor wanted to increase the dosage. I couldn't believe my ears and I knew intuitively that something was definitely not right with that advice! I chose to get off the Prozac immediately, as I was becoming suicidal, and experienced yet another horrible withdrawal.

A week later, I was actually in the middle of asking my husband for a divorce and during that conversation the telephone rang. It was his sister, telling him that his father had suddenly passed away. I don't think anyone will ever understand how awful I felt in that moment. The guilt that rained down on me was almost unbearable. I immediately withdrew my request for the divorce and went to the funeral with him. And I remained with him for several more years. I even returned home one more time after the divorce.

The Entrepreneur

I want to touch on the fact that during all of this time of difficulties in my marriage, I was working various jobs and had started several businesses. I felt that if I could at least succeed in business, then I'd have proven to everyone that I was worth something. My husband and I had gone through bankruptcy after my son's surgery and were always struggling financially to make it. My hopes and aspirations were fueled by a belief that I could fix everything if I could only become a successful entrepreneur and make a lot of money. I'd always loved business classes in college and loved the thought of being self-employed like my father.

Needless to say, the victim consciousness did not work synergistically with creating success in this realm. In fact, several of my businesses failed and one of my business partners committed fraud, which cost me a lot of money, heartache, and time. I had also made some very unwise choices on my own that caused the failures. These experiences fueled my low self-esteem and made life even more difficult for me.

The Stalker

To make matters even worse, during all those years of pain and troubled life, a man was stalking me. To this day, I have no knowledge of his identity. From the time that my second son was born and through the following nine years, I received disturbing phone calls at all hours of the day and night. I'd be changing my baby's diapers and run for the phone, and it would be this creepy voice making a lot of sick comments to me. We changed our phone number, but he still found us. He even called the telephone company on Halloween one year acting as if he were my husband, and had the phone shut off! We set up security codes to deter it from ever happening again, yet he somehow got our phone number again. It was then that the local police began an investigation. He'd phone the house when we had babysitters and tell them that he was going to come and get them. Needless to say, it was traumatic for them, too. He'd find me wherever I was and torment me. He seemed to know where I was, and whenever my husband wasn't home he'd call more often. One night, my husband had gone out ice fishing overnight and, of course, he called me. He also somehow had got wind that I was supposed to be going up to my parents' home with my sister one weekend. At the last minute, I had decided not to go. She informed me that he had called for me at my parents' home that weekend! He called me at work regularly and even harassed one of my employees. After the police did catch him (via a trace) in the first year into the experience, they told me that he was a minor, so they weren't able to disclose his identity. No charges were ever filed against him. I was informed that the police detective went to his home and spoke to him and his mother. That same afternoon he called yet again! He then started calling and doing a clicking routine on the phone to let us know that it was him, yet not enough times within the 48 hours needed to trace him. He'd occasionally call from pay phones and then speak, even leaving some horrible messages. I can't even begin to tell you how many times I'd just collapse on the floor in tears from the fear and stress of that young man's cruelty. When my husband asked him what he wanted with me, he stated that he wanted to . . . (I can't write the swear word here). It was especially fearful for me that he knew when I was alone at home or at work.

Eight years into this drama, our babysitter's sister decided to play "copycat" and believe me, she got caught. Fortunately, when Caller I.D. came onto the market, the police gave us one of the first units, and the ordeal finally ended. I cannot tell you how relieved I was when it was all over. It took years to shake off that experience and still—to this day—it unnerves me.

Giving Treatment Another Try

Throughout the years that followed my father-in-law's death, I worked hard at saving my marriage. I had periods of time when I felt better (healthwise) while attending various weekly 12-step meetings for eating disorders, seeing a psychologist, and seeking guidance from the pastor at my local church. I had felt emotionally stable on and off for the next few years, although the eating disorder would flare up regularly. I loved being a mom and did my best to try to lead a more normal life. But the marriage was still in deep trouble and we separated several more times.

My faith in ever getting long-term help had really begun to waver again. But I didn't quit trying to find it. Instead I found the courage within and I persisted. I had little children, and if not for myself I would keep trying to get well for them. During the next seven years, I sought out and tried even more programs, including completing a 28-day inpatient program for eating disorders in southern Wisconsin. None of them were able to bring me long-term healing and all were missing the core of the problem.

I believe that I wasn't able to heal fully because I was both misdiagnosed and had not discovered the powerful effects of amino acid therapies at that point. I also wasn't able to get into a personal relationship with God outside of religious beliefs, or find any deep sense of spirituality. I was working the programs, going to meetings, and still couldn't seem to beat the disorder and the depression that came with it. During yet another separation, I met a man, got pregnant, and had an abortion. More guilt and shame from the religious connotations brought me even further into despair. I even went back to my husband during that time. And things grew worse.

It wasn't a pretty picture. When the confrontations began to flare up in front of the boys, I knew that I had to leave, if not for myself, then for the children. I was afraid that my boys would end up being the same way when they grew up. I had very little money and had to go on assistance from the government. This added to my already low self-esteem. I at last filed for divorce from my husband after the birth of our daughter. I continued to take every step that I could think of, including turning to religious guidance on many occasions to improve my life. I always felt like God was somehow punishing me. I thought that it was for not living my life the way that I was taught growing up in the Baptist religion. I thought that maybe I deserved it. After all, I never could quite live up to the expectations of the church or my family, and I couldn't see myself ever doing so.

My soon-to-be ex-husband convinced me that a joint physical custody arrangement was better for the children because he had money and a steady job. The love of parenting my children had always inspired me to keep seeking to be a better person, to always seek more help when I needed it, and to keep as much of a positive attitude as I could, no matter what life threw my way. It was incredibly devastating to only have them part-time and even more difficult to watch my ex-husband use the children to hurt me on a regular basis. Not long after the divorce hearing, I attempted suicide for the first time in my adult life. I ended up in the hospital and the psychiatrist came to the conclusion that it was post-traumatic stress syndrome from losing full custody of my children.

I somehow kept going and with the help of my parents was able to purchase a mobile home only a couple of blocks away from my children. This seemed to help immensely, as I was able to be more stable, work, and have my children far more often.

Ancient Revelation

In 1995, James Redfield's book *The Celestine Prophecy* arrived in my life. It was a book that jump-started the process of remembering who I am and removing the layers of darkness that had blinded me to my true self, my true nature. Its words foreshadowed my personal awakening process. It resonated so strongly in my soul that I couldn't put it down. From the moment I picked up *The Celestine Prophecy*, I realized a newfound willingness to look at life from a broader perspective. There was much more to life than I had been taught, and someone was writing about it and shedding light on many of the special gifts that I always knew I had. What a relief!

I began to pay attention to synchronistic events (others call them coincidences). I soon noticed that other people who also believed there is far more to life than what we can see, touch, taste, and hear began appearing in my life. For the first time, I began exploring belief systems outside those I had been given as a youth. In fact, I became hungry to learn all I could.

Around the time I was reading *The Celestine Prophecy*, I met Tom, who would become my second husband. Due to the complicated nature of this new relationship—including bringing together his children with mine—there wasn't a lot of time for me to invest in my newfound spiritual interests, but those new beliefs were never far from the surface.

That moves our story forward to 1998, when I experienced the near-death event. At that time, I was in utter despair. The landlord that had assaulted me still had the key to my apartment and could show up at any time. The antidepressants prescribed by my doctor months earlier were doing nothing to assist me. In fact, I felt even more nervous, flat, and empty than ever. Unlike in previous suicide attempts, I gave no indication to friends or family of what I was about to do. I was living on the edge and had desperately attempted to get help through my health insurance company, but, like many other people, I had a hard time getting my insurance company to cover my treatment program of choice for the eating disorder that was destroying my body and my spirit. They wanted to send me to a traditional program that I'd already been through many times before.

It had only been three short weeks after the sexual assault in the laundry room of my own four-plex, my home—and I was still in anguish over what I should do about it. I did attempt to find some normality and support my kids in their lives. I had gone to one of their hockey games, where I ran into another hockey mom whom I knew from years earlier. Halloween was approaching and she invited me to a Halloween party hosted by another hockey parent.

Now, mind you, it had been seventeen years since I had attended an adult Halloween party and I knew deep-down inside that I needed to get out and be with people and not be sitting at home by myself feeling so distraught, so I agreed to go.

The night arrived and I asked my friend and neighbor to help me figure out what I was going to wear and she gladly assisted me. She, too, was very worried about my well-being and was glad that I was going to go out and actually do something for myself. I dressed in a Cat in the Hat outfit that my friend had given me, and drove over to my hockey friend's home to catch a ride to the party with her and her husband. As my friend finished getting ready, I visited with her sons and their friends who had arrived to spend the evening with them. I really enjoyed visiting with that particular group of young high school girls and began to cheer up. One young woman really took to me and we enjoyed a very nice conversation.

We headed over to the party and I, like the others, poured a drink and began to talk and laugh at one another's costumes. I was so happy and appreciative to be out and about with other people in such a festive environment—and for the first time since being assaulted had my mind completely off my troubles. I was laughing and actually having fun, when the friend that I'd come with approached me and looked terribly distressed. She told me that she had received a phone call from her neighbors and was told that the police were at her home because some other neighbor had called them about an underage drinking party.

We left immediately and when we arrived at the house, two police officers were there interrogating the kids. My friend was visibly upset and crying and I walked with her past the police officers as she went in search of her sons. I immediately observed that one of the female police officers was very angry and seemed to me to be speaking extremely harshly to the kids. I actually recognized this officer and realized that she had been at my own home earlier that year when I had called the police because my then-drunk husband was going to throw my computer and other office equipment out the window. It was because of his anger that I had moved out. I also remembered that she hadn't showed any compassion whatsoever at my house that day. She had told me abruptly and point blank that it was marital property and that there was nothing that she could do about it. *Period.* Obviously, that memory wasn't a fond one—and to hear her speaking in such a crass tone to these kids disturbed me. This time it wasn't me that she was being cold and rude to, it was some very young and frightened teenagers.

I just couldn't help myself. I looked at her and stated "that she didn't have a right to be speaking that way to these kids," but before I could say another word she reprimanded me with a sudden sharpness that I will never forget. I instinctively did as she said, and I went into the house to find my friend downstairs speaking emotionally with her son. He was distraught and apologetic. I felt that I had better let them speak alone and went back upstairs.

Once back upstairs I felt the tension and observed the chaos going on all around me. I looked to my right and observed the same police officer admonishing one of the girls severely now—the same girl that I had been having such a nice visit with earlier in the evening. That was it! I couldn't stand it. The emotions were very high in that house and I was feeling them intensely. I walked over to the officer and blurted out once again that I felt that she had no right to be that abusive, to be treating the girl that way. The officer turned to me and with a vicious and penetrating look of rage in her eyes (one that I was unfortunately very familiar with from an abusive ex-husband), said in a very uncompromising way, "That's it, you are under arrest." I couldn't believe my ears! She hollered to the other policewoman to come and cuff me and the next thing I knew, there I sat in my Cat in the Hat costume in the back seat of a police car, accompanying the kids (some of whom were my son's hockey teammates during the years he was growing up—they were now on varsity and he on J.V.). Finally, I was shoved disrespectfully into a cell at the local jail. I was humiliated and, frankly, soon became hysterical at this shocking turn of events. I thought, *my God*, I am sitting here in jail for standing up for some young girl. And the man who had just turned my world upside down by assaulting me at such a vulnerable time in my life was probably at home in his warm bed with his naïve wife!

I think every single bit of rage from the painful wounds that I had stuffed deep down inside myself for years, the ones that I now see had been festering inside me since childhood, came to the surface . . . and I began screaming. I used every single bit of profanity that I'd ever heard. I couldn't have calmed myself down if I'd tried. Anguish and agony would describe those feelings well.

And no one came to help me as I sobbed uncontrollably in despair. (You can only imagine the shame, guilt, and self-judgment that surfaced a day later when I realized that my son's former teammates were in the cell next to me!) My mind kept replaying thoughts like, "Could I be any more pitiful, disgusting, and unworthy of my love, especially of my children's love; you are worthless; you deserve to die; this life isn't worth living; your children deserve a better mother; my ex-husband was right, I asked for it, I'm crazy, I hurt my kids by leaving him and breaking up the family; I am a sinner; it's all my fault"—the tape just played over and over in my mind.

But the story gets worse. Due to my distressed behavior, rather than try to calm me down, the police officers decided to send me to the county detoxification center a good ten miles from where we were. Mind you, I was tested, and was *not* at a legal limit—not even close—for alcohol toxification. This is where it moved from a nightmare to experiencing the closest thing to the description of the bowels of hell that I had been given as a child in church!

This detoxification center was once an old sanitarium, and please realize again here, as I mentioned earlier in the book, *I was often aware of when entities were around me*. Ever since the out-of-body experience, I seemed to have a far keener sense of negative energies (call them ghosts, whatever you prefer) and this place was full of them! I had never before in my life felt such a cold, dark, and heavy sensation as I did the night I attempted to fall asleep in that place. Yes, I was now sure—*I knew what hell was and I was in it!* I thought, this is it. I am sure that I am being punished by God for all of the bad things that I had ever done; every bit of ill will and every sin that I had committed was unforgivable, and this was all I deserved from life.

Wait . . . there's more! The second night that I was there, I could distinctly feel the beings. In fact, there were even actual cold spots, which any ghost expert will tell you are signs of where an entity's energy is, and they were all over the room that I had walked through in order to get to my cot. Quietly, in the dark, I asked others in the room if they felt it, and several of them answered absolutely, unequivocally, YES!

As I was finally drifting off to sleep after hours of praying to God for forgiveness and help and protection, I was awakened. I heard what sounded like a man's voice coming closer to the room. Now, this was an all woman's floor and the gruff malelike voice was growing louder and louder. The room was dark, with barely enough light to make out a figure. I heard the attendant tell this person to sleep in a cot near mine. I was very upset but afraid to say anything. After the attendant left, I saw this large person get back up out of the bed and crawl into the bed of a young teenage girl. She screamed and the attendant came running. When the lights were turned on during the scuffle, I saw that the "man" was a large, rough-looking girl with short spiked hair, who had a very raspy low voice. The young girl was terrified over what had just occurred and I comforted her. I was a mom by nature after all, and I just automatically become the nurturer in times of need like that. The other woman was then promptly escorted out of the room.

In the wee hours of the morning, we all slowly drifted off to sleep and then were awakened again quite early by a member of the staff. As groggy as we were, we could clearly hear that what she had to say to us wasn't good news. She informed us that not only was the rough-looking girl coming back that morning, but that by law, and for health reasons, she had to notify us that this girl was infested with scabies and that we would be exposed to it!

I was stuck there for 72 hours. I had no money for an attorney and was placed into a group of others that were in the same unfortunate distraught mindset that I was. And, frankly, some even worse off who were going through drug withdrawals. I had called my friends frantically to help me get out of there and they could do nothing. Hell? Yes, I think that I could say I have experienced hell.

Hindsight is often 20/20 and now, as I share this very traumatic and painful experience with you in this book, I can observe the chain of events without reliving the pain and I realize fully that it did happen for a reason. But, at that time, when I was finally released and sent home to explain it all to my children and ask them for forgiveness, I was still in a very traumatized and degraded mindset.

Now, in late November of 1998, I had given up hope at every level of my existence and felt that my life would never change for the better. Even my sales skills did nothing to sway the insurance company from their limiting rules and regulations; I was unable to obtain access to a treatment center that I believed would help me overcome my bulimia and depression. I had researched like crazy on the Internet and found several holistic programs that gave me some hope, but they would not approve any of them. I was heading into the darkest time of my life. Fear, guilt, shame, and failure were in my consciousness as I sank deeper into despair.

The Near-Death Experience

Perhaps you, too, have experienced such despair, such hopelessness. I felt that I had no choice, no hope of getting off the treadmill of trauma that had formed my life up to that point. My body and mind were filled with the remembered anguish of sexual assaults, abuse, and poverty. I had reached my breaking point. I didn't feel that I was good for my three children. I felt I was putting them through a hardship once again, with another divorce and yet another move. I didn't feel like I was being a good parent who could provide them with security and a happy, prosperous lifestyle, as their father claimed he did. My children's father did everything he could to put me down and let me know that I was a failure, for he was still bitter about the divorce. It seemed as if there were no hope. A darkness fell over me, unlike anything I'd ever felt before, filling me with deep, relentless frustration and anguish. This time, I was going to end it all. I so wanted to "go home," to find peace on the other side, in what I had been taught was a beautiful loving place called "heaven." Enough of the misery, suffering, pain, and guilt.

It was early afternoon when I left my suburban home near Minneapolis. I hadn't been emotionally able to work on my home-based business and had quit the airline job not long after the assault. Depression left me overwhelmed, and the assault by my landlord, in my own laundry room, left me an emotional wreck. I just couldn't handle the pressure anymore. I had been cooped up in my apartment for more than a week, not going anywhere and fearing that my landlord would return at any moment. Like many sexual assault victims, I was afraid to report him. I had no money to move out and therefore felt completely helpless in being able to find another place to live if he evicted me.

A surreal numbness overcame me as I stopped at a neighborhood liquor store and bought a pint of tequila, and then walked out of a drugstore with a box of sleeping pills. I envisioned finding a deserted place in Wisconsin, just across the Minnesota border. I was not sure exactly where I would end up. I drove until there were no houses around, to a place where I would not be noticed. I turned down a gravel road behind a small hill and stared blankly out into a field. I stopped the car, shut it off, and proceeded to drink that tequila straight, downing the pills in between with a diet soda. It wasn't long before I felt myself fading off, and so I decided to crawl into the backseat and fall asleep to my death. I remember experiencing a strange grayness, darkness . . . and then out of that darkness emerged three robed men. They began speaking to me. I found it strange that I could hear them speaking, but I did not see their mouths moving. It confused me, yet as they drew nearer to me, I began to feel a penetrating and profound knowingness, compassion, and even a bit of sternness in their communication to me. They informed me that it was not time to leave my earthly experience, that I had made a contract that was not to be broken, and that I was needed on the planet. I recall pleading with them, telling them that I couldn't handle it anymore, that the pain was too great, and that I wanted to come home. My feelings of sadness and hopelessness were met with an even deeper, pulsating sensation of compassion and a profound and penetrating feeling of love that words could never describe, emanating from them directly to me.

I didn't experience the beautiful white light many people speak of in their accounts of near-death experiences. There were no pretty fields of flowers and beautiful lakes. That lonely evening, I simply met with those who reminded me of the importance of my contract to be here on this planet during this time of great change. I still remember resisting their strong promptings, arguing that I could no longer stand the intense emotional pain. I remember telling them over and over that I wished to "go home." With all my heart, I tried explaining and pleading with them to let me "die now." Yet their sincere compassion and powerful love flowed out to me in a way that I had never before experienced. It embraced me, enveloped me, and, slowly, I allowed myself to absorb it. I remember agreeing with them and acknowledging my contract, with some resistance at that point, and then feeling a complete knowingness with all of my being that they were correct. At that exact moment, when I understood that I must go back, when I agreed to go back, I was pulled through a tunnel of energy that sucked me back into my body. I awoke with a jerk and instantly became fully conscious.

Feeling ill and full of panic, I looked around. By that time, it was dusk. Though, obviously, hours had passed, I knew that I needed to rid my body of the pills and alcohol I had ingested. I immediately threw open the door of my car and induced vomiting, an ever-so-familiar behavior after 19 years of bulimia. I also knew I needed immediate medical help. I tore out of that farm field and, to this day, I still have no recollection of driving until I saw flashing lights in my rearview mirror. When I pulled my car over, an officer came up to my window and explained that I had been speeding. A few moments later, he asked me to step out of my car. Even though I was still dressed in my black business suit, I must have been a mess. Probably suspecting I was under the influence of something, he proceeded to have me touch my nose with my pointer finger and stand on one foot. He gave me a Breathalyzer test. To his surprise, I did not test intoxicated. I also did my best to convince him that I was just fine.

I could have driven off down the highway at that point, ticket in hand, had it not been for the deep, patient, and sincere compassion shining through his eyes that night. He did not walk away. He stood there as if an "angel" were gently encouraging and prompting me to seek help through his eyes. When I think about it now, a wave of gratitude for his assistance still wells up inside me. Within minutes of finally explaining to him that I had tried to end my life, I fell into a confused and semiconscious state in the back of an ambulance that he had called to the scene.

We Meet Again

A year or so later, a gentleman I was dating decided to surprise me and take me to his friends' home to treat me to an authentic Tibetan dinner. I had met the hostess previously and was delighted to see her again and to savor her cooking. After enjoying a delicious meal, I was led downstairs in this home where a temporary monastery had been set up to meet some exiled Tibetan monks who had recently arrived from India. Because I had been exploring world religions other than Christianity, I was especially delighted to be experiencing their beautiful culture and this type of worship.

The Dalai Lama was scheduled to arrive in Minnesota within

a few short weeks, and the monks were preparing artwork and gifts for the event. The younger monks were working on beautiful art pieces. They were sculpting, molding, and detailing them intently as I walked into the room. They smiled and we enjoyed a brief introduction.

After soaking up the peaceful, loving energy in that room, I glanced over to see an older monk sitting cross-legged in meditation. To my utter astonishment, I recognized the monk's face! Instantly, at the deepest level of my being, I felt as though I were being pulled back to that near-death moment in the back of my car in the isolated landscape. The peaceful monk in front of me had been one of the robed beings! The intensely powerful, loving energy flooded me once again, and I was speechless. He smiled back at me, acknowledging my presence and seemingly aware of my recognition. Not a word was shared between us that evening, though the connection was amazing. I stood there for a moment. When my friend began to lead me away, I followed him back up the stairs. I sat down in the living room with my friends, feeling utterly blown away by the experience. I excitedly told them the story. Needless to say, it took a while to calm down from the excitement and shock. No one there seemed at all surprised. That incredible experience confirmed to me that my choice had been correct when I agreed to come back to this present life. Life is indeed full of miracles, and I felt like I had certainly just experienced one.

The longing to be fully enlightened, to remember all of who I really am, and feel on a daily basis the depth of love and compassion that I experienced during that near-death experience, has yet to leave me, because until this cycle is complete, it is all but impossible to quench the thirst that I have to be whole again. I yearn to be reunited fully with the peace, harmony, bliss, and joy that I now understand reside within the inner connection to one's soul, to the Creator of All That Is. I am that I am. I yearn for the unlimited potential that resides in the freedom of living in that Divine will, the Divine connection that frees one of all restrictions and pain.

For in that pain was where I agreed to go in search of self. The pain truly became a tool, a key, to finding myself once again. Becoming able to accept that pain, and to forgive myself for wanting to take my life, has been a journey of desperate seeking and, in fact, a longing so intense that it propelled me to find my way home. The desperation was unbearable at times and sometimes, in my blindness, I sought relief, begging to go home. I came so close, throughout the years, to leaving this place. Desperation gave way to hope on more than one occasion, as death evaded me more times than I care to admit. If it hadn't been for my guides and angels, I surely would have succumbed to the very human nature that I so wanted to save.

Events of my life have taken me through several unexpected detours, but I ended up back where I was supposed to be, on a healing path co-created with my higher self and God, and shared with you in this book. This path is one that leads to higher consciousness and personal transformation. And like James Redfield, I also believe that this is an accelerated time of transformation for humanity on this planet.

This is a time when the focus is building to transform and evolve the human consciousness. It is a time of revelation, manifesting the truth foretold by ancient prophets of many world religions. Yes, the time has come to reveal the truths, to offer the option of saving yourself, and to assist others who walk here beside you. The story is NOW, and the reality of time is fading as we near the amazing transformation of human consciousness itself.

For me, the journey has been worth it—and actually, it has just begun. The memories of the pain are leaving me. Just like when a mother holds that babe to her bosom for the first time, the growing joy alleviates and heals the memories of the recent pain of childbirth. In a far broader, more universal sense, that moment is upon us. It is time to enjoy the warmth and nurturing of this new Earth ourselves and leave behind the pain. As I proclaimed, shortly after my last suicide attempt, "I won't be a victim anymore!" I truly live *now* from a place where I am a victim no more.

2

Our Four Major Life Challenges

The truth is that our finest moments are most likely to occur when we are feeling deeply uncomfortable, unhappy, or unfulfilled. For it is only in such moments, propelled by our discomfort, that we are likely to step out of our ruts and start searching for different ways or truer answers.

—*M. Scott Peck*

The four major challenges that we face in life are relationships, abundance, health, and self-worth. These issues are interrelated and feed off each other in many ways. These "challenges" bring forth the underlying fundamental lessons that we face as spiritual beings living a human life on this planet. They inspire us to address what it takes to find spiritual enlightenment and fulfillment while facing the day-to-day tasks as a human being. The more I identify with these four life "challenges," the more I realize how all of these areas actually are constantly interacting and overlapping with one another in our daily lives. I can see clearly now that by bringing these challenges to light, our soul is asking us to give our attention to these areas to become whole and complete, to live in this world without being of this world.

Each of these components is equally important and requires equal attention. I believe it is vital to address the self-worth challenge first and foremost, as a lack of self-worth is responsible for our feeling of separateness and robs us of our joy. A lack of self-worth also creates the victim consciousness, and it dumps our lives into a world of chaos. You will find that when you address and heal this area of your life, it becomes the catalyst for success in finding balance throughout life.

The issue of self-worth is woven throughout this chapter's exploration of relationships, abundance, and health. The chapter concludes with a final comment on self-worth, saving the best for last.

Relationships

I became well aware early on in my conviction to heal the victim consciousness that my lack of self-worth was feeding the struggle and chaos I was creating in all my relationships. This lack of self-worth was affecting my relationship with family, friends, and mates alike. My self-worth was so low that I was drawing in others to treat me at the same level that I believed I deserved to be treated. The men in my life at that time didn't make for a pretty picture. And on that note, working to free myself of the habit of judgment has probably created the most positive change in me, by huge leaps and bounds.

A lack of self-worth and self-love left me with few or no boundaries to speak of and, as a result, I let my emotions "rule the roost" in choosing whom I'd attract into my life as a lover and/or mate. Of course, along the way, I set some limits. After my first marriage, I decided not to live with someone who would abuse me the way my first husband did. But when I fell for (and, believe me, that is a good way to phrase it) my second husband, the same underlying situation and set of circumstances were cloaked in a different form. This man had a different personality, yet the underlying issues were still there to be dealt with. Although I'd done a little group therapy after my divorce, I hadn't worked on healing my own underlying *guilt* issues. You see, I still believed, as a Christian, that I had failed with my first marriage, not quite lived up to doing everything that I could possibly have done. I felt guilt, shame, and self-blame which left me unhealed, and so I was destined to repeat the same old lesson until "I got it."

You see, I just couldn't fathom living life without a man in it. I loved the fairy-tale feeling of being married and caring for someone, and living happily ever after. Just as in *Cinderella*, I was waiting for my prince! I wanted to recreate this magical dream world for myself. From that perspective, having someone to take care of me seemed only right. In the society in which I'd grown up in the late 1960s and 1970s, that was the way we were told it would be.

Going Down the Old Familiar Path Again

When I attracted into my life a man who had recently lost his wife—she had been a stay-at-home mom, and that was what he was used to—I thought that I had found my miracle, a new chance at the fairy tale. The chemistry between us was amazing. My emotions were in ecstasy! He seemed nothing like my first husband in personality and demeanor, and I loved that about him.

We met at a hockey game (his son had become friends with mine). He seemed interested in my new studies and was supportive and open-minded about me stepping away from my family's traditional religious upbringing. He hadn't been raised in a strict religious family and seemed to understand my desire to discover my own beliefs.

That summer, my younger son was on a baseball team with his son. I broke off a long-distance relationship and Tom and I began dating. We married within eight weeks of our first date (obviously an emotion-based decision, wouldn't you say?), while I was on a business trip—and it felt like a dream come true! I was sure in that moment that I was going to have my fairy-tale life after all, even if that fairy tale started in a wedding chapel in Las Vegas. . . . Thank goodness I still have a sense of humor, as it makes sharing this story much easier!

At the same time, I had also bought into the dream (and had been working on this dream for years) of being an independent woman who was perfectly capable of becoming a successful and wealthy entrepreneur. I had observed changes in our society as a result of the women's movement, and those changes really caught my attention! Ah . . . the insanity of being raised in the 1970s. It seemed that many women still wanted the fairy-tale relationship, while at the same time desiring to have one foot on the other side of the fence as well. When I met my second husband, he seemed attracted to this dream and intrigued by my desire to be independent. That excited me even more about this new relationship. Once we married, however, that dream came crashing down.

He wanted me to become successful and wealthy, but he also wanted me to care for our house and the five children, have dinner on the table when he got home, and not be working on my business after hours. It didn't take me long to become overwhelmed by trying to feed both of these dreams. I watched the fairy tale go down the drain.

I was dealing with the emotional issues of two stepchildren who had lost their mother less than nine months earlier, moved across the country, and suddenly had a new stepmother and three stepsiblings in their lives. And my children, who still dreamed that their father and I would reunite, were forced to make adjustments related to moving once again, having their mother remarry, and feeling the obvious disapproval of their own father. Chaos grew and grew. The different values of these two families that had merged also became more and more pronounced as time went on. My husband began drinking more often and smoking marijuana on a daily basis. He threw himself back into gambling to deal with his own frustrations. Everything seemed out of balance, and I began to spiral out of control myself. I drank along with my husband, began overeating, and gained 60 pounds within the first year. The former bulimic behaviors returned with a vengeance, as I lost all hope of saving my business.

My husband and I separated, and I moved with my kids into a small one-bedroom apartment. After being stood up by my estranged husband at least two dozen times, and subsequently being sexually assaulted by the landlord, it took that near-death experience and the healing that followed to wake me up to the fact that I had a belief that I didn't deserve anything better in a mate than what I had already experienced. It was time to let go of the fairy tale and the notion that some white knight was going to come save me. I had to find a way to save myself, and, by God, I did! I am here to tell you that there is a way of creating a fairy tale in relationships, but it's up to you to create one with yourself, a fairy tale of your very own first, and one that is based on a new set of tools and healthy self-worth. Once you take the time to heal yourself . . . then and only then will you draw someone to you who will bring you peace and happiness. As you learn to love and respect yourself and set your boundaries in a way that honors you, you may find that your mate may respond accordingly. If not, you will have all of the tools necessary to come to an enlightened and logical decision in Divine order.

Blaming Others Is Just Excusing Yourself

When we are still in the early stages of our healing process, we are quite prone to blame others. We've been doing it for a very long time and it will resurface. Count on it . . . and be willing to release it as it comes up. Release it, and replace it with higher thoughts and feelings of peace and love.

Quite often, as a result of old habits or patterning, we tend to blame our partners for more than their fair share of problems that cause breakups. To make ourselves feel fine with our decision to end a relationship, we tend to overstate the perceived flaws of our mates or friends. We do this to justify our decision, because we are still practicing our new way of being empowered. We are not used to feeling worthy of making decisions that are for our highest good, and therefore we can fall back into the blame game very easily. Just be aware that you may do this and own your part in the whole experience. As you remember to release judgment of yourself and others, there will be no need for blame at all.

Fear of rejection also arose during my healing process. I've come to understand that as I had rejected myself over the years through self-judgment and lack of self-worth and love, I also created reasons for the men in my life, family, friends, and even my children to reject me. I would set myself up to be rejected because I was rejecting myself. This is an example of the mirror effect. The world was a reflection of me on many levels, and this certainly applied to relationships in my life. I can also see clearly that this fear is lessening as I move further into my healing process. I've begun to trust in my own ability to set boundaries and love myself more deeply, so I am now more willing to risk the chance of being rejected by men. Because my self-worth is no longer based on whether or not I have a man in my life, I am able to set boundaries more effortlessly when dating, and I can trust that I will no longer allow my emotions to decide whether I take any relationship further. This has allowed me to be willing to give dating a chance again.

I realized that I had to change myself before I could draw in someone else who could mirror a beautiful and healthy relationship. I admit that I have had times of loneliness, but with each relationship I've had, I've learned something beautiful about myself. I never dated as a young teenager, as I was extremely overweight and unhappy, and so now I am getting the chance to get to know what it is that I want and don't want in a life partner. I've read plenty of books on relationships, such as *If Love Is a Game, These Are the Rules,* by Chérie Carter-Scott, and made a list of what I want in a mate. And, for once, I am being patient and waiting for this person to show up in my life. I also examine any feelings of chemistry, which create emotional responses, through my logical self. That, in and of itself, is a pattern that gives me hope that some day I will feel safe to be in a relationship again.

Making a Change in My Friendships

As you heal, frankly, you may also outgrow some of your friendships. You will begin to see that what you've settled for from these friendships is no longer working for you. You will also grow to understand that what used to work for you in a particular friendship does not anymore. When living in the victim mindset, often the first thing you do when meeting someone is share your wounds. In fact, this is more common than not in our present social structure and culture. I learned that if I continued to hang around people stuck in the negative drama cycle, the more I tended to be pulled down emotionally with them and stay stuck in that cycle. It is as though the marshmallow effect took over (i.e., focus on the negatives in life and they will grow bigger). Another tidbit here: I now understand the old adage "Misery loves company."

The contrary effect became obvious when I was drawn to read materials that shared the positive messages of wisdom such as "success breeds success." Spend time with successful and happy people and that is exactly what you will begin to draw into your life. More success, and more happiness! I applied this wisdom and, much to my own joy, began to build new friendships. Today, I am blessed beyond boundaries with amazing new types of friendships and still have been able to maintain some of my older ones, in a wholly different manner. I am drawn into friendships that center on my spiritual healing and all of the positive aspects of that process, rather than on the old pattern of sharing wounds. I now apply my top priority of living free of the victim consciousness to my selection process with my friends. I have the following poem framed and on a wall at home, as it is a good reminder to have while you are on this journey.

Some People

Some people come into our lives and quickly go. Some people stay for a while, and give us a deeper understanding of what is truly important in this life. They touch our souls. We gain strength from the footprints they have left on our hearts, and we will never ever be the same.

—*Author unknown*

It is important for you to understand (and be aware) that there will be changes in your friendships as you heal. Be aware that as you grow to new levels on your healing journey, people will come and go in your life. This will help you anticipate change and assist you in preventing unresolved feelings from robbing you of your desire to attain positive goals in this life challenge of "relationships."

Having this realization helped me deal with memories of past relationships. One of those memories goes back to my senior year of high school. I had begun a crash diet in the latter part of my junior year, and by that fall when I returned to school, I had lost 80 pounds. It was the first time in my school years that I hadn't been obese. For years, I had habitually been putting myself down to avoid being put down by others. High school is difficult enough to navigate when you're healthy, and even harder for someone as emotionally vulnerable as me. For years, I had the hope that if I would only be thin, my problems would all go away.

So here I was, thin for the first time in my life, and my group of friends was in for a rather big shock when I returned that fall. You see, I was no longer willing to be the butt of my own put-downs. I had changed my outward appearance, and I expected them to accept the new me—period! The result was I had to let go of the old excuse that "others don't like me because of how I look." That was a biggie! I wasn't emotionally prepared to let go of that excuse either. Friends of mine had to deal with all these personality changes in me, and also deal with someone who was as excited as I was to have lost the weight. I was wrapped up in all the new feelings going on inside me, and I couldn't stop talking about the change. It must have driven them crazy.

Eventually, they let me know how this affected them. One day at lunch, they all sat down with me and, one by one, told me what they thought of the new me. Among the long list of complaints, they felt I had become a people-pleaser, was obsessed with my weight, and always was talking about myself. Maybe some of it was true, but it wasn't a pleasant experience. In fact, it traumatized me. But, once again, it was all part of the process, and that experience inspired insight and healing later in life.

A wonderful thing to remind myself of occasionally is to be very grateful that I am not in my adolescence anymore. (Humor comes in handy!) The teenage years can be a harsh and difficult experience. Often the damage done then can take many years to heal . . . but oh how it can make you a stronger human being for having made it through that time. Many successful people share stories of teenage misery and the pain induced by peers in school. They also share how those experiences motivated them to prove everyone wrong!

Let's apply the same technique to our lives here and now. Remind yourself that the trials and challenges of life lead you to go within and discover your own peace and happiness. Everything happens for a reason, and that includes your relationships.

Discover Clues to Your Old Habits by Looking into Everyday Events

Let's look at something as simple as how we interact in our own friendships. A friend of mine recently shared an insight that made a whole lot of sense to me. She said, "If you want to see which friends you are closest to, pay attention to who is doing the calling." This "assessment" is actually a great test to see if you've been needy and have been using "force of will" in a friendship. When we are feeling vulnerable, we often may fall into the habit of being needy and rely far too much on our friends in our decision-making process. And whether we realize it or not, we may use a type of "force of will" on our friends by inadvertently imposing on the friendship. Often we do so (use force of will) by using guilt on them when they don't want to listen to our problems at the moment, or even by manipulating them with our "poor me" attitude and trying to make them feel guilty if they aren't helping us out as much as we think they should be. Victims can be very manipulative, getting their way even if they don't realize it. I did this in the past.

We all have old habits that we are shedding as we move out of victim consciousness, and this may just be one that you need to look at. If your life has been filled with chaos on a regular basis and you didn't have the tools to deal with that chaos on your own, you may have been, unbeknownst to you, projecting your problems onto some of your friends. In fact, as I mentioned earlier in this chapter, often when we meet people while in the throes of drama-filled lives, we are drawn to those who have the same kind of energy as we do. More common than not, we tend to share our wounds before anything else when we meet new people, and that is how many of our old friendships were born. Keep in mind that it is also easy to give your power away to your friends. If you are constantly asking for advice, or giving advice for that matter, rather than simply sharing the more joyful experiences in your life, you may have developed a pattern of unhealthy dependency on your friends, or they on you.

Sure, there are challenges in life, and it's nice to ask for advice and support, but are your typical conversations focused on this "co-dependent type" of negative interaction? Pay attention to what you talk about when visiting with your friends on the phone.

Are your conversations pleasant and focused on positive events, or is there a habit of sharing each other's woes or is there a whole lot of complaining going on? Let's take this further: If you are doing all of the calling and this person has a habit of not calling you back, you might want to take a look at whether you are imposing yourself on someone, rather than having a healthy reciprocal relationship. Or is it the other way around? Do you have someone always calling you to complain and commiserate? Do you have a tendency *not* to want to call them back? Of course, you don't have to apply the "all or nothing" attitude with this exercise and jump to assumptions. I suggest that you take some time to write about it and you will draw a more logical conclusion from a more objective viewpoint. Journaling, by the way, is a wonderful healing tool.

Learning Some Effective Communication Skills

First, take the opportunity to get a wider perspective of the situation and get out of your emotions, and then discuss the results of your assessment with your friend without any shame, guilt, or blame in the conversation. Beginning your sentences with "I feel" is the best way to engage in a healthy discussion. Many of us were conditioned to using the blame terminology in the victim mindset, such as starting sentences with, "You make me . . ." or "You are so . . ." We are learning to take responsibility for our behaviors and to find new ways of changing our daily lives. There is a great program that Marshall B. Rosenberg, Ph.D., developed called Nonviolent Communication (see www.CNVC.org) which teaches remarkable techniques in learning to have non-threatening and healthy conflict resolution.

In fact, the world is opening up with support for you now that you are becoming aware and letting go of the old ways of doing things. There are so many wonderful resources available today that can help you build very empowering ways of communication. Of course, John Grey *(Men Are from Mars, Women Are from Venus)* has given us some key insights to the male/female relationship dynamics. Something as simple as learning that women are more emotional in their communication, and men tend to be more logical, really helped me in the way in which I interact with my male friends and my sons, for that matter. Now that I am aware of those differences, I don't take it so personally when a man responds in a more typical "male manner."

Use Your Imagination

Samuel Taylor Coleridge once stated that "Imagination is the living power and prime agent of all human perception." And I agree wholeheartedly with that statement! We all have wonderful imagination skills. You can even pretend or imagine having fun and healthy communications with your friends. Don't judge yourself. Again, make light of it and have some fun with it! Practice with a little role playing, or for that matter, now that you are becoming your own best friend, practice with yourself in the mirror! You can even get some kicks and giggles with role playing. For most of us, using your creative imagination came natural to you as a child; why not put it to work and have some fun with it as an adult. Laugh at yourself, play and *dream big*. See and feel yourself becoming a wonderful friend to others and they to you. Feel what it's like to have them call you! You can become the teacher in the relationship. As you become more effective with your own communication skills and patterns, others will begin to respond to your new techniques.

Again, it just takes some practice. I've learned that my way wasn't always the best way of communication in the past. Why? Because, as I've mentioned earlier in this book, I had a limited viewpoint and was extra sensitive from all of the hurt and drama that I had created in my own life.

Always look at the bigger picture. Remember, the awareness of a habit brings with it the opportunity to change it if it isn't doing you any good. You have a choice; in fact, you have more choices than you ever thought possible.

Now, please don't just assume that because you are doing all

Our Four Major Life Challenges

of the calling the other person doesn't want to be your friend. You may have just gotten into the habit of interacting that way. I am simply encouraging you to look at some of these assessments and options from a higher perspective with these suggestions. In order for you to learn to access different patterns and areas in your life, why not practice with your close friends and let them know that you are exploring some new skills in creating a happier, healthier lifestyle and you want to start with your friendships. If they truly are your friends, I would think that they would be open to helping you and maybe learning something new that will make their life better as well. Just don't jump to any brash decisions; practice taking your time and be gentle with yourself and others. Do this before making any major changes in your friendships! Remember, we are releasing the all-or-nothing patterning, and we're adding logic to our toolbox.

We also have to consider the dynamics of passive and aggressive personalities. Some of us are aggressive and some of us are passive. Opposites often attract. The key is finding a balance. If you tend to be aggressive and your friend is passive, look for a middle ground and settle in there.

Use these tools to create your new happier relationships. Applying common sense in all areas of your life is important. Also, remember that very few people can read your mind! May I suggest that if you are unsure whether a present relationship is fitting into your newfound "victor mindset," do the following exercise:

- Make a list of what assets you bring to a friendship (for instance: I am open, honest, dependable, and generous).

- Next, make a list of what you feel the ideal friend would be like (for instance: thoughtful, honest, open, caring, and dependable).

You will most likely see that the lists match up, but if they do not, then it may be wise to do a little work in this area. Get clear on what you want and don't want, and then you will be more apt to attract that to your life. Discuss this list openly with your friend and see what you both can do to compromise. Use this list also in manifesting new relationships.

Because of low self-worth in the past, it is common to compromise too often on our own good. As we began to heal, it is wise to reevaluate and take a look at compatibility issues in our relationships: Are my needs being met? Am I giving more than receiving? I highly recommend that you get clear on what you want to give and receive in a friendship and then practice asking for what you want. Open and honest communication between friends is important. It is not wise to make any assumptions in relationships. Don Miguel Ruiz's book *The Four Agreements* is an excellent source of wisdom in creating healthy friendships.

You Have the Ability to Handle Whatever Happens, Even with Your Family Members

We often have the most difficult time with our family members; in fact, sometimes even more so than with all other relationships. Family members seem to be able to push our old hot buttons more easily than anyone else. Many of us have painful memories of our childhood experiences with family members; however, I can't stress enough the importance of honoring yourself first and foremost. Don't expect miracles to happen overnight. I want you to know that healing myself has changed the dynamics of the relationships with my parents, siblings, and children. I now experience more joy-filled holidays with them. And, after I was able to let go of my resentments and hurts from the past, it became far easier to interact with all of them. Now, it takes some time to get there, but when you do, you'll find that they aren't able to push your buttons like they used to! And, although I don't see them as often, because of distance, I have a more natural and healthy interaction with them. As I've grown more self-confident, I no longer require their approval of me, and that has changed how I interact with all family members. I work to no longer make assumptions or accept their criticisms. When I am not feeling strong or in a state of mind to interact with my birth family, I choose not to go to a gathering. I have learned that I have to honor myself before others, and that seems to work for me. Also, with purpose and with love, I have had to discontinue regular communication with a particular family member. I still care deeply about her, but I simply find the old way of interacting with her to be detrimental to my healing process. Of course, I did my best to communicate my needs to her prior to changing our relationship. But when she didn't choose to respond in a positive manner, I decided that I would let it go for a while. Often, time and space will heal a relationship; other times, we just learn to detach with love. I trust that, as with every other part of my healing process, time does heal all. I then let it go and, once again, trust that it is all in divine order.

As for my children, I cannot express how much better my life has been with them since I committed to free myself from the victim consciousness. I know that they have seen great changes in the way I live my life. By that example, they see a whole different way of approaching life and many different options that they can choose to adopt in their own lives. I am honest with them in sharing that I am responsible for every choice that I've made, and I let them know that I am still working on myself.

The time that I spend with my children now is far more rich and beautiful than I ever dreamed possible. My sons are now over the age of 18 and my daughter is now in high school. I look forward to continuing to share my life with them and being an example of someone who has chosen to live in a state of higher consciousness.

As for my personal friendships, I chose to leave some of the unhealthy ones behind. I have had to go through the grieving process of doing so. Now, I am blessed with many friends who resonate with me in my new way of life.

There were times along the way to finding this new circle of friends when I was lonely. I used those times, however, as an opportunity to know myself better and fall more and more in love with who I am as a human being. I've noticed that my friends, old and new, are far more patient with my progress on this path. I am sure that reflects the fact that I've learned to be my own best friend. I am happy just being with myself.

Abundance

When I felt guided to write about life's four major challenges, I winced at the thought of writing about abundance. In fact, "Oooh and ouch, do I really have to?" was more like it! Why, you may ask? It was because the first *form of abundance* that I thought of was money. And, as a child, I absorbed many beliefs about money that were then incorporated into my own belief system, and those beliefs did not create a positive experience in the financial area of my life. In the dogma of my religion, money and greed were often referred to as one and the same. Believe me, I've learned to change that belief and now it has changed my entire experience in my relationship to the energy of money.

As I've worked to learn about how to relate to and accept abundance, I've found that many other light workers seem to have this challenge in their perceptional field hanging around to be healed. I've also learned that many of us are challenged to release vows, contracts, and covenants of poverty from former lives as healers. In past-life regression sessions, I learned that I had lived three lives in which I was very wealthy, but I had abused the way in which I had achieved the wealth. In one of those lifetimes, I even took my own life as a result of feeling guilty for abusing my power while I held a powerful position within a church and all but stole the church followers' money through trickery and misuse of the teachings of the Bible. Three other lifetimes shown to me in an intuitive reading were examples of times when I lived in extreme poverty, one to the point of starving to death on the street. What I learned from these sessions was that I am here to heal that energy. I am here to find balance and freedom, to forgive myself, and to release judgment of where I've been. I am here to claim the unlimited source of abundance that is available to me through the Creator.

Yes, there have been times when I achieved financial abundance. I had projects that did very well and I was able to draw in some nice chunks of cash at various points in my career. A pattern always repeated itself, however: I would not be able to keep the flow coming nor honor myself enough to think about my "future self" in using the money that had arrived. Often I felt that "this was it," that I had finally stepped into the flow, developed the momentum, and was sure that it would continue. Funny, but it didn't. The same "come here, go away" mentality that I had with relationships and self-acceptance manifested itself in my financial life as well. I couldn't figure out how to keep the success going, and it frustrated me like crazy, to say the least!

A Message That Was Disheartening but Ultimately True

A very successful businessman told me one time, years ago, that I was one of the most brilliant and talented people he had met, and that the project I was working on most certainly had the potential to bring me the wealth I was seeking. Much to my disappointment, he ended the conversation with one more comment: that, in his opinion, I was not in the right frame of mind or "place" to handle the wealth that could come from it. Needless to say, I was angry as I walked out of that office that day. I felt as if he had stabbed me right through the heart. Why? Because underneath that facade of brilliance and confidence I was projecting, I knew he was right. It has taken me a long time to understand what he really meant. I am here to share the secret, the wisdom on abundance that was shared with me that day. The fact of the matter, and the truth underlying his message, was that *I had a lot of healing to do in my life*. It was a definite task that I had to accomplish before I could truly accept success into my life for good. I really was not ready for a windfall of financial success at that point in my life. I had a big task in front of me first, a more important priority, and that was to leave victim consciousness behind. I needed to find the skills to live a life of empowerment rather than letting my desire for financial success overpower me. I wanted to prove myself to others by becoming financially successful and that just wasn't the path I had chosen.

I cannot emphasize this enough. Regardless of the form in which success manifested—be it happy and healthy relationships, good health, or financial wealth—the only way that I would realize it on a long-term basis in my life was by accepting my worth and by truly and wholly loving myself, unconditionally!

Most of us associate the word "abundance" with finances, period. I was one of those people. I've since learned that abundance comes in many forms. The act of *practicing gratitude* in my life, while on this healing journey, has assisted me in understanding this.

Finding Gratitude in the Lessons of Living in Poverty

As for applying gratitude, I want to share here another example of the blessing of accepting "Divine timing" rather than "Lori's timing" in my life. It's another example of "hindsight is 20/20." As I write this, I can now say with all my heart that I am glad that I went through those years of poverty. Why? Because as I spent time gathering and researching additional information for this particular chapter, I ran across yet another gem of wisdom in *Spirituality for Dummies*, which I mentioned earlier. In the chapter entitled "From Greed to Divine Abundance," I read the section on "Blessed are the poor" and became excited when I realized author Sharon Janis was describing what I had learned from going through my own experience of poverty. She taught, as do I, that "poverty can definitely open up new pockets of appreciation." Please understand that neither Sharon Janis nor I advocate poverty in our teaching, but we both seem to agree that *gratitude* is one of the most powerful tools in the healing process. In my "tool chest," I place it right behind *releasing judgment*. Here are a few of Janis's points that really jazzed me when reading them and affirmed my perspective on why I chose to use poverty as part of my healing process and growth experience.

- Poverty can be a great tool for taking complete refuge in the present moment. It can also help you develop greater surrender and faith while you sweat it out.

- Poverty increases your compassion for yourself and others. Often the poorest people are the most generous to others in need.

- Poverty gives you greater appreciation for what you have and for whatever small blessings you receive.

I've clearly seen that, as I've healed and claimed my divinity, I have grown to appreciate a new and greater abundance of friends, healthy relationships with my family members, and more peace of mind from having gone through this struggle with financial abundance. It made me become a more compassionate, giving person overall. I also have a greater appreciation for the type of work that I am able to do now with my writing and for my accomplishments since I decided to live free of the victim mindset. As I grow, heal, and base more of my decisions on logic, I am clearly heading in the right direction with finances. Why? Because I know that I am worthy!

I also have come to discover that I can attribute at least 90 percent of any of my present stresses to this "category" of financial abundance—connected to my sense of worth—and have set forth my intention to fully claim my healing in this area now.

I also remind myself that I had underlying issues of low self-worth when I played out the victim role, sabotaging my own success in many areas of life, finances being one of them. My low self-worth and beliefs about money were tied to each other.

As I began the process of setting my goals to become financially free, I realized that, to attain that particular goal, I needed to take into account another priority I had set forth. And that priority was my desire and determination to live a life free of the victim consciousness. To achieve both of these goals simultaneously, I had to apply the new principles and tools I had learned in living free of the victim mindset in every area of my life, and in proper order. One of these major principles or tools was "to know myself and my limitations."

As I began to reorganize my "thought process," and looked at how I made all my life decisions (including adding logic to the formula), I realized that I needed to look at my "Priority List." I had to identify whether or not the new financial goals I was setting honored the rest of my healing process. Many books that share practices of those who have become financially successful speak of these individuals as having a desire and persistence, a driving force behind all of their efforts. Their desire to achieve financial success became the number one priority of their lives.

I pondered this as I read Napoleon Hill's book *Think & Grow Rich,* and I quickly realized that what I was reading was aligned with the set of principles I have been sharing in this book. Having a burning desire is a key factor in becoming successful at anything. I compared the burning desire to being godlike; Mr. Hill related it to the goal of being financially successful. Clearly, a burning desire can be applied to any goal one wishes to attain, and it is important in this conversation to look at all four of life's major challenges and determine where that "burning desire" energy can be applied.

Another similarity that I found, in Napoleon Hill's book and in many others, was adding the ingredient of "persistence" to manifesting financial wealth. Persistence has never been in short supply in my life, but what I found myself objecting to as I read further was identifying financial success as my number one priority. I was not willing to replace my top priority! What I soon discovered is that the planning I was doing for my financial success had to take into account my real-life situation. I had years of conditioning in the victim mindset and I was still working to free myself of those old patterns.

The old "all or nothing" mindset of victim consciousness was conflicting with my new goal of living a balanced and peaceful life as a spiritual being in the area of finances. Aha!

The beautiful gift in this whole process of finding answers to achieving financial abundance was seeing clearly that I was already applying my newfound set of principles and priorities to planning and processing in my life. Yet I needed clarity on exactly what financial abundance was to me, how it fit in with living a life free of the victim consciousness, and how to develop a solid, step-by-step plan to achieve balance in all areas of my life.

This excited me, and I pondered a recent situation involving an acquaintance. I observed a woman with a deep desire to start another new business. I clearly saw what she was doing. Yes, she had the burning desire to attain more abundance, but at what cost to her own healing process and her relationships with her children and friends, let alone her health? I could see that this new venture was affecting all other areas of her life in negative ways.

I began to apply these observations to my own experiences. I began to understand that each and every time I had set out to start a new business, I had also had a burning desire to prove to others and myself that I could be financially successful, and I had not looked at my overall goals. This was a huge insight to me. I felt myself literally healing by shifting my viewpoint on how I would find success in all areas of my life as a whole. No longer was I seeking financial abundance to prove anything to anyone. I would create abundance by honoring all of who I am, as a spiritual being living a human experience, and develop that plan in a sensible and practical way.

I haven't lost one bit of the passion or excitement of achieving financial abundance. On the contrary, I am more excited than ever! In fact, the passion is growing, as I can now see that meeting my financial goals will be much more fulfilling and joyful than ever before. At long last, I now know that I will be in a place of balance, serenity, and peace in all areas of my life, and that will enable me to appreciate fully the beauty of realizing that I am worthy of all the blessings, in every area of my life. That now includes financial freedom. The financial freedom will not be at the expense of some other area in my life, for it will truly work in harmony with my spiritual life purpose and enhance the rest of my priorities—in a sensible way, I might add!

I highly recommend reading *Think & Grow Rich*, but before doing so, understand that Hill's insights about achieving abundance need to be applied first and foremost to your healing process of shedding victim consciousness.

Financial abundance will surely follow as you grow to love yourself unconditionally and live free of the old patterns and beliefs that brought you so much discontent and unhappiness before you decided to own your empowerment as a spiritual being—a spiritual being who is part of God.

God is love, and love is abundant in this universe.

Figure 2-1. Creating an even flow of our time and life energy, giving equal time and energy to each of the challenges, is important during our healing process.

Figure A: If one area gets too much of our energy—the other areas suffer and we become unbalanced.

Figure B: As you see in this figure, if we distribute our time, attention, and energy equally to these four major life challenges, we find balance in our life as a whole.

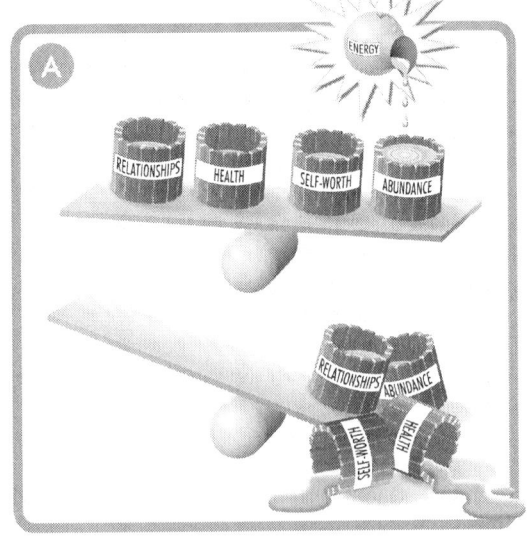

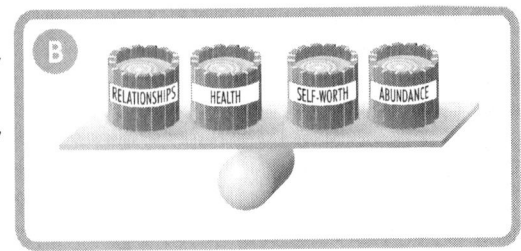

Health

I love sharing the results of my healing process. Prior to the emotional healing that allowed me to rise out of the victim mindset, the stresses of living in the victim consciousness were evident in my thick medical file at the local clinic. Most doctors are well aware that stress causes many forms of illness and it most certainly did for me.

Eliminating Stress

I believe that it is important to keep the body-mind-spirit connection in view. Believe me, the body takes a beating when the mind and spirit are wounded from living as a victim. The stress of living on that *drama treadmill* took its toll on my physical body in many ways.

According to Stephanie Marohn, author of several of Hampton Roads' Natural Medicine Guide books, "Chronic stress wreaks havoc on the body, mind, and spirit and creates a vicious circle. On the physical level, stress drains nutrients and lowers immunity. The nutritional deficiencies result in compromised neurochemistry in the brain, which in turn reduces the body's ability to cope with stress. Lowered immunity also reduces the stress-coping capacity and opens the body to the development of disease. In addition, it creates disturbances in the energy system of the body, which affects all levels of functioning."

Living in the victim lifestyle produced all kinds of stress in my life on all levels. Frequent moves, arguments with spouses, sharing custody of my children, divorces, sexual assaults, and financial strain all caused tremendous stress to my body and I was ill often. I even had four surgeries in the five months just before I made my mental and spiritual health a priority in my life. My doctor has been amazed at how rarely I have had to visit him over the past five years. I am sure that he has seen firsthand through my case that healing the mind heals the body.

I advocate incorporating integrative medicine into your life. I stress "integrative," as I believe that utilizing both conventional and alternative medicines is highly effective.

Wonderful naturopathic doctors and programs that emphasize the body-mind-spirit connection are available to us. Universities are now adding alternative medicine to their medical degree programs. The University of Minnesota is one of them.

One of my first experiences with herbal medicine came after I fractured my sacrum (a large bone located at the base of the spine) in a fall on the hotel steps while on a business trip in Salt Lake City, Utah. It was a very painful experience and taught me how a fraction of a second can change one's life significantly, as happens with a sudden physical injury. After several months of recuperation, I was still having extreme pain when I sat for long periods of time. Since I was a hockey mom, that was a big problem. I shared my feeling of frustration with my mother and she mentioned that both she and my sister-in-law had been helped dramatically by an herb called yucca stalk (from the yucca cactus found in Arizona). I decided to give it a try and, much to my amazement, within several weeks of taking this herb, I was able even to ride a bike. I felt like I'd experienced a miracle. Sharing my story about the sense of miraculous healing that followed taking yucca stalk prompted many others to share similar stories with me.

In the United States alone, the herbal supplements industry has grown into a billion-dollar industry. Why? Because herbal medicines work and have been used for centuries all over the world. In the Far East, herbal medicine is still one of the main forms of medicine. American doctors are beginning to pay more attention to it as well. I've met wonderful naturopathic doctors and herbalists who have dedicated their careers to teaching their clients and the public about the benefits of using this form of treatment. Dr. Andrew Weil is quite well known in this arena.[*] As another benefit, the herbal medicines

---

[*] My publisher, Hampton Roads Publishing Company, has an entire line of books that can educate you about so-called alternative medicine. See its website at www.hrpub.com. You can also search on the Internet and you will discover myriad websites full of wonderful information and assistance if you are interested in this area of medicine. Or visit your local library for more information.

I've taken are far less expensive than the pharmaceutical prescriptions I purchased in the past.

When reading *The Mood Cure* and *The Diet Cure* books written by Julia Ross, M.A., I thought that I'd actually hyperventilate (okay, I'm exaggerating a little here to make a point, but it was a *huge relief* to discover this information). I read case study after case study about her patients who suffered from the same symptoms that I had for years! I was even more relieved to know that many of my emotional and mental health problems were actually caused by amino acid imbalances—very simple to correct. I know this for a fact now, because after I started her supplement program, my symptoms went away. I never realized that I could feel so, well—normal! I had seen very positive (and sometimes huge) leaps forward in my emotional state from incorporating the tools that I share in this book, but this program became the icing on the cake. I cannot recommend enough reading and applying the information from these books. To give yourself such a powerful gift as to follow through with Dr. Ross's recommendations would be one of the greatest rewards of reading this book. When you can begin the process with a more even mental-health state, it will make applying the other tools that I offer here far more effective and productive.

As I moved out of the victim consciousness and got into the habit of *not giving my power away,* it created another big change in the area of my health. I wasn't so apt to do whatever the first doctor recommended to me. I would explore opportunities, trust in my own intuitive senses about my body, and get second opinions if I felt guided to. I've noticed others taking on the role of a more assertive and self-educated participant in their own care, as the basic structure of healthcare in the United States has been going through tremendous reform. With so many Americans without health insurance, many haven't had an option but to do so. I have also made it a point to exercise more, eat healthier, and drink more water than I ever did. The healthier my mind and emotions grew, the more I desired to take care of my body. To summarize, I've found that the more I raise my energy into the light, addressing and healing the emotional garbage that seemed to wreak havoc in every area of my life, the less disease has been able to attach to my body. The more I honor my healing process, the more I am guided in caring for my body in a reverent way.

In so many ways, I see how all these life challenges interact with each other, and that when I move to the next level with my financial abundance, I will have the opportunity to indulge myself with even more preventive healthcare.

Self-Worth

Self-worth has been addressed throughout this chapter—for good reason. The entire theme of this book is about learning to live free of the victim consciousness, living free of the judgment. It all comes down to loving yourself unconditionally. The only way to achieve this is to own your empowerment and own wholeheartedly that you are worthy. You are worthy because you are an amazing spiritual being! Nothing, be it personality, predisposition to emotional sensitivity, things you perceived you've done wrong, or any other circumstance that hinders your happiness and fulfillment, can take away the fact that you are an aspect of God. You are living and breathing, growing and evolving, and experiencing the gift of life in the best way that you know how, in this moment. You are worthy, you are worthy, and you are worthy! Say it aloud: "I am worthy."

There is nothing that you could do or say that will separate you from the Creator. Within you lies the seed of your divinity, and you are certainly well on your way to awakening it. By reading this book and committing to making the choice to live free of victimhood, you are automatically setting the energy in motion for your awakening. Choose to no longer see yourself as separate from God, and accept your worthiness. You can create the life you long for.

Making Some Rhyme and Reason Out of Our Beliefs

I believe that we are born into this world in innocence. We adopt the beliefs of our people and society as we grow and evolve. We really don't have a choice as a child to pick and choose what we want to believe. We are all taught beliefs that are "good" for us: for example, that burner is hot, don't touch it or you will get burned; you have to stay out of the street so that you don't get hit by a car; you need to behave in school so that you don't get in trouble; study hard and you will get good grades; etc. And I venture to say that everyone is also taught various beliefs that just don't align with our own innate nature and fall short of being "good for us." There are limiting beliefs, such as: you cannot become a doctor because you are not smart enough; you shouldn't hang around that person because they come from the other side of the tracks; and you don't have a right to change your mind. As we enter our school-age years and move on into our teens, we begin to form some of our own beliefs outside of our family's teachings (for some, this also includes questioning religion). Often this is seen as rebellion, and much to the dismay of our families and church leaders, we began to form our own attitudes and beliefs about life. Our peers begin to influence us even more as we enter our junior high years, as does the media. Often our families use guilt, shame, and blame in trying to get us back on track and so the power struggle begins.

A Course That Changed My Life

"Avatar" is a course that teaches "what you believe is what you create." Three months after my near-death experience, I attended a Woman's Expo in Minneapolis and was drawn into a booth that advertised a self-development program. A kind and soft-spoken woman asked me a couple of questions that got my attention. I had never heard about anything like Avatar prior to that day, but let me tell you, bells and whistles were going off like crazy in my mind. And I sensed strongly that I was right where I was supposed to be (the old intuitive nudge at work). It turned out that stepping into that booth wasn't a coincidence. I signed up for the weekend course and somehow managed to manifest the money for the weeklong course. That program changed my life more than any other traditional therapy ever did! Avatar, a course produced by Star's Edge International, offers a series of experiential exercises that enables you to rediscover yourself and align your consciousness with what you want to achieve, and it changed my life entirely. Taking this course actually allowed me to truly understand that I had held a belief that I was *not worthy*. In fact, I discovered that I had adopted (took on a belief that was projected out to me) a belief that I actually hated myself. Yes, you read it correctly; I actually held a belief that I hated myself while doing one of their exercises!

Understand here that an indoctrinated belief is one that we do not consciously realize that we have taken on. It is a belief that we "bought into" subconsciously at some point in time without even realizing it. As I mentioned earlier, we are all indoctrinated or "taught" by our families or society to believe the way they think we should. It is a natural part of life. And just like wearing sunglasses, sometimes we tend to forget we are wearing them. With some beliefs, we don't realize that we ever put them on in the first place. When an indoctrinated belief doesn't align with our own underlying beliefs, it causes all kinds of disturbances in our life. Often, the negative beliefs that we buy into harm us in many ways. Remember, we are all born on this earth innocent and come from the source of love. God is love and that is probably why we so often hear the saying from new parents that their baby is a "gift from God."

Now, for me, realizing through that exercise that I had a belief that I hated myself made some sense. Why? It is because, as the youngest of six children, I had memories of rejection for as long as I could remember. Memories flooded in of my siblings telling me that I never belonged in their family. They would tell me I was different from them. I never fit in because, unlike them, I was hyperactive and talked nonstop. As an adult, I have since discovered that a chemical and nutritional imbalance was the cause of that behavior. But as a child, it was just natural for me to buy into the spoken beliefs of my siblings.

No, that did not surprise me at all, for my life choices reflected a lack of self-respect, self-love, self-esteem, and self-worth. Interestingly, once awakened to the fact that I had this disempowering "invisible" belief, I also realized that I had knowingness, deep within my being, of a great love for the precious being that I am. You, too, will learn to fall more and more in love with the beautiful light that is within you as you continue on your journey!

A Special Exercise for Connecting to Your Higher Self

One of the techniques that helped me to connect with the light within was an exercise described in the Lazaris material in *The Sacred Journey: You and Your Higher Self,* written by Jach Pursel. In this exercise, you imagine you are sitting under a huge tree. Your higher self is on the other side of the tree. Reach your hand around the tree and place it in the hand of your higher self. Stand up and look him/her in the face. Now do whatever comes to mind. In my case, I was just so happy to see my higher self that we danced together, hugged each other, and swung each other around like two little girls playing the spinning game. From that moment on, I felt a special relationship with my higher self. When a love song came on the radio, I sang it to her. I would return often to that tree and reunite with her in my mind. I knew that I was never alone. I guess you could say that this was the way that I was able to truly fall in love with all of myself. Self-worth grows very rapidly when you find a way to do this.

And by the way, when you can avoid judging yourself, you can accelerate the process greatly.

3

Returning to Logic

> Every adversity, every failure, and every heartache carries with it the Seed of an equivalent or a greater Benefit.
> —*Andrew Carnegie*

Victim consciousness is prevalent in our society. It is the premise and foundation of the old paradigm that we are about to leave behind. No longer is there a need to be the victim, the victimizer, or the rescuer, for that matter. We have an option now that allows us to choose a process of awakening to self-love and unity, releasing our old negative patterns, and integrating new, more positive thoughts and actions. The accelerated healing process of the higher vibrations is now available to us because of a new and growing awareness of our higher selves, our spiritual selves, as well as all of the other extra help from light workers that is available to us. With holistic medicine and other healing modalities gaining acceptance in addressing the physical, mental, emotional, and spiritual issues, we can speed up our healing process so much more. I will discuss some specific healing modalities in the later chapters of this book. Keep in mind that there are many different modalities available which are effective in achieving results in certain areas of our health and well-being. All modalities of healing are energy or love, and come not from the facilitator but from God; the facilitator is only the conduit.

Healing modalities range from traditional Eastern-based medicine to more scientific allopathic medicine, which is what we know as conventional medicine, as well as many areas in between. However, not every modality is appropriate for every person. This is because we are all unique and individual, and the type of healing that will be effective for one person may not be for another. The effectiveness of any one modality is largely dependent upon the openness and the ability to receive of the person requiring the healing.

The Process of Healing

The effects of healing are not always completely predictable. Repeated treatments may be helpful or even necessary in order to obtain maximum benefits and for effects to be longer-lasting or permanent. It is rare for complete healing of a problem to occur in a single treatment, though not impossible. Don't discount the possibility, but keep both a balanced mindset and a positive outlook while pursuing your healing.

Healing is usually a gradual, gentle process that brings about changes on many levels: spirit, body, emotions, mind, relationships with other people, and relationships with the environment. You may continue to experience benefits from a single treatment or a series of treatments over a period of weeks and months and even years. Healing is not necessarily always about curing symptoms or diseases. The process may just help you understand how to live with your problems and deal with them better. There may be a variety of things you can do to facilitate your own healing, such as changing lifestyles (diet, exercise, meditation, learning what your symptoms may be reflecting about your life, dealing differently with stress).

With that said, for many of us living in the thick of victim consciousness, our lives tend to be driven by our emotions. I was a pro at letting emotions take control when making many of my decisions and, frankly, it was because life simply felt illogical. I couldn't make sense out of what was happening in my life as a child. I associated logic with how things made sense. I was told that God is love and it made no sense to me that I had to do certain "things" to win God's approval. Furthermore, I was taught that I would be punished if I did not comply with the rules that had been set up for me: attend church at least twice a week, no drinking, no swearing, no smoking, no dancing—and on and on the rules went. The Baptist church in which I was raised taught that there was the right way and wrong way to reach salvation.

I began learning about other religions through friends at school, and I discovered that they had other beliefs, based on what they were taught by their churches and families. So what was going on here? Who was right? Who was wrong?

Losing My Grasp on Logic

I just couldn't understand what caused me to be punished in such awful ways. What on earth had I done to deserve being traumatized at the age of 12; an elderly man cornered me in the barn. He fondled and kissed me and told me that the neighbor girl did this with him and I should too. I was shocked and fear welled up inside me. I even became physically sick. The whole experience made no sense to me. What had I done to deserve this? More fear and confusion followed when I told my parents about the incident. Instead of supporting me and insisting that I was not to blame, they dismissed the event as if nothing had even happened. I felt as if I were all alone and no longer protected by my parents—and that made no sense to me. My parents and my church told me that if I did things their way, God would protect me and keep me safe. But this violation, and my parents' refusal to even acknowledge it, eroded any sense of safety and self-worth I had. Logic? At that tender age, I found no logic in what had happened to me. Furthermore, the deep depression that followed this incident made logic a fog of frustration and a haze of self-rejection and disgust for years to come. After that incident, I alternated between being despondent and admittedly angry and defiant. My emotions bounced around like crazy and not much made sense to me in my life at all.

In hindsight, it makes sense that as a result of such childhood incidents, I adopted a belief that if something made me feel good, I should follow it. When I was feeling bad, I acted out or ate it away. To heck with running it through a logical thought process. I just wanted to feel good and know that I was going to be okay. And when I ate things I liked, and when I would withdraw or act out, I was able to have some level of control in that moment. I am aware now that I used food to soothe my emotions so that at least something made me feel better at least temporarily. My mother was a stress eater and I watched for years as she did the same. Again, I no longer blame my mother or father for any of these experiences. It was all a part of my life lesson, and I've grown much stronger as I've learned to turn the pain around and become a happier, more compassionate person for having gone through all of the aforementioned struggles and having the ability, through drawing on love, to change my life.

What I did lose during my childhood, though, was a crucial part of the healthy, decision-making process. I lost a willingness to apply logic to my decisions. It took me many years to see that I needed to return to believing in this thing called logic, that the thought process of finding sense in everything was an important process. It was a necessary step to stop the cycle of drama (see figure 3-1).

The process of making victim consciousness decisions:

Idea + Emotion = Poor Decisions

Figure 3-1. Practicing instant gratification or anger-based responses creates a reactive and unhealthy decision-making pattern, *which often leads us smack-dab into more problems.*

Decision-making process for someone
who is living in "victor-hood":

Idea + Emotion + Logic = A Healthy Decision

Figure 3-2. This type of decision is made from an expanded or "higher level" of consciousness. This kind of decision-making creates proactive decisions rather than reactive decisions.

When a victim begins to step out of the blame game, and no longer judges himself or herself, a willingness to make sense of life returns.

The beginning of the return of logic, and things making sense to me, came early in my healing process of coming out of the victim mindset. Two powerful insights were instrumental in my transformation. As I absorbed these insights, they eventually became a part of me, an intrinsic part of my knowingness. These two insights were the beliefs that "there are no coincidences" and "everything happens for a reason." These two phrases became my first "tools," and they brought me peace when I felt life was making no sense at all. Inspired by my life experiences, and by reading *The Celestine Prophecy*, I began to notice, time and time again, that I had a lot of synchronicity happening in my life. There were no coincidences, no accidents—only signs from the universe that all made sense in hindsight.

The ideas "everything happens for a reason" and "hindsight is 20/20" work well together. It was getting easier for me to look back on my life and see the countless times I had wished for or prayed like crazy for something I wanted to happen, only to be more than relieved later that those prayers or wishes had not been answered. Garth Brooks's song "Unanswered Prayer" is a perfect example of this truism. In this song, Brooks sings about attending a football game and running into an old high-school girlfriend, a girl whom he had prayed to have for his wife years before. In this song, he shared that he was so thankful that his prayer wasn't answered, because now he realized that he and this old girlfriend didn't have much in common. Garth also realized that had his prayer been answered, he would not have married the woman who was now his wife and mother of his children, whom he loved and adored. Some of life's greatest gifts are unanswered prayers.

My tool chest of mantras began to replace the negativity of the past, and I soaked in the wisdom that they inspired. I began to notice some positive changes occurring in my life as I continued to heal. I had gone through the pain, stepped off the drama treadmill, gained some clarity, and developed new beliefs that aligned with my inner knowingness (my inner truth). I was able to make sense out of many of the situations that had occurred in my

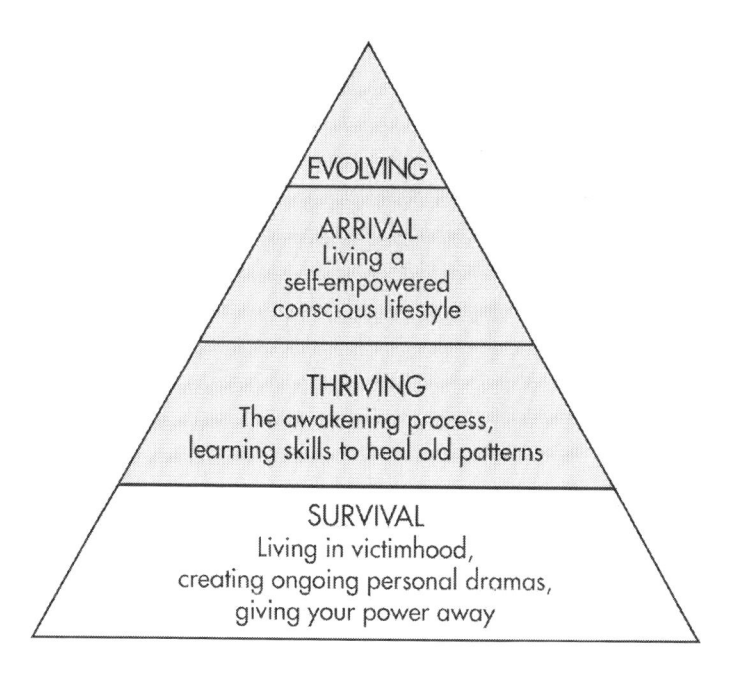

EVOLVING

ARRIVAL
Living a
self-empowered
conscious lifestyle

THRIVING
The awakening process,
learning skills to heal old patterns

SURVIVAL
Living in victimhood,
creating ongoing personal dramas,
giving your power away

Figure 3-3. I chose the structure of this chart to symbolize that each level of the process is equally important. We move forward in life. But spiritual evolvement in this process is not a hierarchy. It is simply learning to move forward in your spiritual life. Honoring and appreciating each level in your process is important.

life, and I began to understand that I was responsible for my choices. There was a higher purpose for my life.

You can see that you are growing and changing, and you can feel that you are living in the higher vibrations of love and light each and every day, through the work that you are doing. Because you are raising your vibrations, you are drawing healthier and happier relationships into your life. Be clear that no one goes immediately from one to ten on the scale of learning to live a Divine life. This is a process, and you will experience transitions from one level to the next, with peaks, valleys, and plateaus along the way. Be realistic about this. Your goal is to evolve from the survival mode, into thriving—free from victim consciousness, safe and secure in your divinity and spiritual empowerment.

Figures 3-3 and 3-4 depict how the healing process occurs. Each of us may experience some variation in the process, but from my point of view, these diagrams offer an accurate summary of what I've observed in myself and others as they've worked toward shedding the victim consciousness. The following details the ten levels represented by the numbers in figure 3-4.

LEVEL 1: You become aware that you have been living in the victim consciousness. You are willing to begin exploring your belief system, make the changes, and step into the process of healing.

LEVEL 2: You choose to make a commitment to leave the old way of living behind you. You begin to take action on that commitment. You apply the tools and insights taught in this book, and you read other books recommended to you or to which you seem drawn. You may sign up for classes or join a group with like-minded people on the spiritual path. You may become ravenous about reading, studying, and learning about the options available to you in creating your unique healing path. Be aware that you are just now beginning to raise your personal vibration, and you will connect with many others who are at the same level. You may be overeager to share all of the interesting things you are discovering, so use discernment.

LEVEL 3: You begin to see the results of practicing these tools and you notice some positive changes beginning to take place in your life. You are finding your own unique way to live out your truth. You definitely want to take this way of living to the next level. You may be led to a particular healing modality to study or a spiritual path to pursue. Some of the old drama cycles are beginning to disappear. There may be "turbulence" in some of your relationships as you begin to change your priorities to higher thought patterns. Others in your life see your changing attitude. Some are supportive. Some are not.

THE TEN LEVELS OF HEALING

1. **Awareness**: Identifying with victim behavior.
2. **Commitment** to change old patterns & begin to practice healing tools.
3. **Step by step**, you begin to see **results** of using the tools.
4. You are now **processing and integrating** new insights while releasing old patterns.
5. The **determination becomes stronger** to create more balance your life.
6. **Increased awareness** of your ability to manifest the life you desire.
7. **Self-worth expands** and grows significantly.
8. You have **stopped creating dramas** and have drawn in mentors.
9. **Confidence** in handling life's lessons.
10. **Experience** more pleasure, happiness, delight, clarity, and peace, in your daily life now.

Figure 3-4.

LEVEL 4: Your desire to live in the higher vibrations leads you to observe some profound changes in your life. You are processing your new insights and investing quiet time to integrate them. Old "stuff" from the past (this life and past lives) surfaces and seeks to be healed. This is when you need to watch for "force of will" patterns. You are releasing much of the old garbage from your life, and you may feel the urge to begin helping others, as well. Be gentle with yourself. Have extra patience with yourself during this time, and don't push yourself too hard. Your old relationships may begin to change in major ways as you become much better at setting your boundaries.

LEVEL 5: You begin to observe and identify areas of your life in which you still wish to find balance. The result of your self-work is becoming more evident, and you are seeing that this work is paying off. "Steady as she goes" at this stage. This is where you really begin to attract relationships that are more uplifting and supportive. Your higher vibrations are now drawing in others who are at the same level and are able to help you continue to grow spiritually.

LEVEL 6: You still experience some residuals of past decisions. Your awareness is expanding, however, to the point that you may be able to observe your patterns while you are actually in the middle of them. You are becoming quite adept at using your tools for self-empowerment and you experience a more positive attitude, even in the midst of chaos and challenge. Humor can be quite effective at these times. You may still occasionally be discouraged, but these times are occurring less frequently. Your desire to fulfill your life purpose is becoming stronger and stronger and clarity around that purpose is quite accurate.

LEVEL 7: You see that your self-worth is growing tremendously and life's "other challenges" want to catch up with the process. You begin to notice this and take action to balance all areas of your life with that new sense of self-worth and self-love.

LEVEL 8: You are an example of living free of victim consciousness. You see that the hard work has paid off. You are better able to navigate in your daily life, without dramas popping up regularly. Your focus is increasingly on your spiritual evolvement. You may seek to master a particular modality yourself on these levels and choose to help others to heal. Issues of survival—dealing with the basic needs of food, clothing, and shelter—do not take up as much of your time, and you are far more receptive to using your intuitive abilities and other newfound "gifts" of your Divinity. You no longer need to judge yourself or others.

LEVEL 9: You accept that the world is right where it is supposed to be, even when something seems terribly unfair and feels unsettling to you. By your willingness to accept that everything is happening for a reason, and by responding in a peaceful manner, rather than with anger at these perceived injustices, you contribute to raising the vibrations of love on this planet, rather than adding fuel to the anger. Have you ever heard the phrase "You don't fight fire with fire"? You truly understand and live this truth by levels 8 and 9.

LEVEL 10: You are aware of your own divinity. Your level of consciousness reflects a high vibration, a level intended for all of humanity. You are well aware of the assistance that you are receiving from the other side of the veil, and you work with your spiritual team—your higher self, angels, guides, and masters—to accomplish your life purpose in a more joyful and peace-filled way. It is a goal that is worth all the effort. The more I explore and question myself on this level, the more I uncover knowledge and discover more questions. I've found that humility is a wonderful virtue to maintain here. Here are the words of two leaders of exploration in our history that describe quite well the importance of humility:

> The more I know, the more I realize I don't know.
> —*Albert Einstein*

> I know only that I do not know.
> —*Socrates*

I look forward to exploring level 10 in my life as I continue on my journey of healing. I may occasionally ebb and flow in and out of the lower levels; however, it doesn't take me long to catch myself and hop right back up to level 10. And I sense that I will be sharing more about this level in my future writings. What I have come to realize is that I am loving and appreciating greatly the fact that I am not only *having the opportunity* in this lifetime *to be aware of this level*, but more importantly, that, along with me, there are many others who are also having the opportunity to maintain an experience in this level of existence. I believe that as more people begin to seek the wisdom of the universe within themselves, the more humanity will benefit from the shift in consciousness that this planet is experiencing.

I've shared the outline of the levels with you because I want you to be aware that you will be vulnerable at the beginning of this process. This is a time when you need to slow down, be gentle with yourself, and start practicing your new tools of self-empowerment. I cannot back off from expressing the importance of *the action* of *"practicing"* when it comes to spiritual development and the process of shedding victim consciousness. I have far too much love in my heart and appreciation for how practicing worked on my path not to stress the importance of practicing and being persistent with yourself and in your healing process overall. And it does take practice to learn to form new boundaries—and learn to honor the new you!

4
Discovering "New Thought"

> It takes a lot of courage to release the familiar and seemingly secure, to embrace the new. But there is no real security in what is no longer meaningful. There is more security in the adventurous and exciting, for in movement there is life, and in change there is power.
>
> —*Alan Cohen*

The Apocalypse and Ancient Wisdom

Apocalypse, you might ask? What on earth does that have to do with learning to shed victim consciousness? Well, frankly, I think it has a lot to do with the state of affairs in our world and the fears that are creating misunderstandings, arguments, and even wars. There are human beings killing other human beings—because they believe that God told them to. One religion after another has fought to be the only one or the "right one" for thousands of years. We are all being affected today by the stress of wars on our planet. From the loss of lives to the environmental damage from the chemical warfare—believe me, we are being affected whether you choose to look the other way or not. Now, this isn't about interjecting fear here; this is about our willingness to acknowledge and confront fear and doing so by stepping into courage. And inside each of us lies an abundance of courage.

Now, I believe that *God is love,* and I've found that belief in the doctrines of most world religions. In one of Neale Donald Walsch's latest teachings, he suggests that we substitute the word "life" for "God" as a unique way of integrating the messages of peace, tolerance, acceptance, and, of course, love in our relationships. I've had fun doing so. When someone sneezes, I now say, "May *life* bless you." People seem to be very open to this substitution; in fact, I've noticed that some people that are put off by the word "God" embrace this substitution. For me, it is just another way of expressing my love to others without offending them.

Victim consciousness is all about choosing fear over love and, let me tell you, if you want to step out of that victim consciousness, then *choosing love over fear is the most powerful way to accelerate your healing process.*

If you truly want to become a happy and healthy individual who loves, cares about, and honors yourself and others naturally, then let's *keep on keepin' on* here. Stretch yourself a bit; use your courage and affirm that you are open and receptive to new ways of viewing life and to expanding yourself to see the big picture with a broader, more positive belief system. After all, if, like me, you took on everyone else's beliefs and truths as your own in your childhood, without even considering your own viewpoint as an adult or revisiting some of those beliefs, well, look where it has gotten you. You are here having to relearn how *not* to be living life as a victim!

The apocalypse, according to the ancient Greeks' definition, is simply "the lifting of the veil." I believe that the meaning of this word has become distorted by humankind's fear into its present connotation of a tragic end and a horrific series of events for this planet. I don't buy into that scenario. In the next few chapters, I share with you some of the more spiritual teachings I've encountered and found helpful in my healing process and spiritual evolvement—*a lifting of the veil of my own belief systems.* We are learning in this book about how not to give your power away, so I once again encourage you, as any true spiritual teacher or coach would, to please just take what works for you and leave the rest behind. I trust that you can do this. I do this myself all the time with everything that I read, whether in a book, in a magazine, or on a website.

I pay attention to the methods, stories, and beliefs these materials and various teachers share, and come to my own conclusion by looking at how I feel when I am reading or listening to the material. I ask myself: Does this feel true to me? Can this information possibly help me to heal the old patterns that were creating misery in my life? Sometimes, I choose just to let go of my logical mind and let my heart tell me if it is good for me or not. I have learned to stay in balance with my logical side, but I also know full well that my logical mind can stop me from being objective and creative. If all of the great inventors, painters, and world leaders had lived their lives by logic alone, we'd live in a very dull world, without the amazing technologies, works of art, and other great inventions we have in our lives today. Not to mention, we'd probably still think that the world was flat!

So here I share some insights that I resonated with, and which helped me find peace of mind and a deeper spirituality in my own life. You, too, may find them helpful.

To Think We Are Limited Only by Our Past Experiences Is Myth

By discovering a broader and more positive vision of what is happening on this planet, I can tap into a universal consciousness of love that stimulates my desire to be more tolerant of others and their extreme desire to subscribe to beliefs about a cataclysmic end to this world. If you think the old ways and the result of our past experiences offer all of the answers, you believe in a myth. We can choose to create whatever reality we desire when we stay in the present moment and positive mindset. In fact, I actually have developed compassion for those who hang on to the past prophecies as if free will never existed to change the outcome. I, too, once hoped that all of my own pain and suffering would come to an end miraculously, in that old blink of an eye moment. I had hoped that I would be instantly transported out of this lifetime into a heavenlike existence on some other planet or in a spaceship or up in the sky somewhere. I could relate to their desire for this to happen, as it actually sounded like a wonderful escape when I was in the thick of my painful victim existence. What inspires me now is embracing life each and every day as a spiritual soul, in human form, that agreed to come to this planet, discover my own divine self within, and develop the ability to create my own heaven here and now or whenever I choose.

The lifting of the veil, the Apocalypse—*the true apocalypse, an expanded awareness of all humans, as prophesied*—will not be diverted. The more each of us expands our ability to experience a more positive and love-filled vision for this world, the more I can see that the plan was for us to shift our consciousness to that of one in which we hold a love and respect for each other. I see the possibilities of applying God-like unconditional love for each other in our daily lives and the opportunity to experience an existence that God always had in store for this planet. I still believe that there is nothing that can stop this divine plan from manifesting, though many have tried to do so, using fear as their primary tool. Escapism isn't for me; living my life in service to myself and others is! Focusing on the fear stagnates and stunts the growth of your healing process.

Focusing on the Positive Events Broadens Your Perspective and Lifts the Veil of Fear

There are rapid changes occurring on this planet; humanity is constantly changing, and with so much new technology available to us, with advancement of global communication through satellites and the Internet, we are all more aware than ever of these changes. You have the opportunity to tune into all of the dramas and negativity that are blasted at you. Or, you can choose the option of getting inspired by looking to the positive news and viewing the many stories portraying the collective efforts of all the people from all over the world (and of many different backgrounds) who are uniting and finding common ground to work on. These are causes such as saving our environment (e.g., bringing awareness to global warming, saving the arctic refuge, rock bands putting on concerts for fighting global hunger and poverty, etc.) and engaging in peaceful demonstrations or virtual marches to rally support for anti-war campaigns. I get so uplifted when I can share in celebrating the victories of these groups and definitely tap into the energy of love when I take the time to participate in them. I see clearly that love *is* the driving force of these efforts. I simply look at those who are caught up in the dramas of negative outcomes as being ignorant of what love really can do when brought together for the highest good of all.

Staying positive means that your focus needs to be on paying attention to letting go of your bad habits and patterns, controlling your own actions, and not reacting to others if they disagree with you. Tapping into the polarities of right and wrong drives people into a sense of separateness and opposition rather than unity. Coming together for the higher good of all creates unity. I have learned that when you judge people for their differences or move away from being tolerant of others' beliefs, you develop a sense of disengagement from those people and God as a whole. As Marty Grothe so eloquently put it: "We can never truly understand people when we hate them, and we can never truly hate people when we understand them."

Life Eternal

What about life on the other side of the veil? I've woken up to the fact that there is a whole lot more out there than what you can see, touch, and feel. Face it, at one point or another during our lives we all face death. And when we do, we began to contemplate our own mortality, especially when a loved one close to us passes over. The topics of spiritual gifts such as mediumship are gaining more notice in the public eye. In the United States, some 50 million viewers watch the popular show *Medium*.

Some people are born with a gift to see to the other side of the veil. Sylvia Browne, John Edwards, Echo Bodine, and James Van Pragh, among many others, have written books about these gifts and the experiences that they have had when using these gifts. Dannion Brinkley also talks about his intuitive gifts being awakened during his near-death experience in his best-selling book, *Saved by the Light*. In fact, they all have been on national television sharing their stories. Many thousands of others have also taken classes from these experts to learn how to use their own gifts, myself included. I took a course with Echo Bodine to learn how to better use my intuitive skills, to help both others and myself more effectively. Actually, we all have that intuitive gift, and it is just sleeping within us. We may call it our instincts or gut feelings. As I mentioned earlier in this book, I also explored books about reincarnation and found that there are some wonderful books about studies of life between lives.

When Dr. Michael Newton, a certified Master Hypnotherapist, began regressing his clients back in time to access their memories of former lives, he stumbled onto a discovery of enormous proportions: It is possible to see into the spirit world through the mind's eye of subjects who are in a hypnotized or superconscious state; also, clients in this altered state were able to tell him what their souls were doing between lives on earth. His book *Journey of Souls* presents ten years of his research and insights to help people understand the purpose behind their life choices, and how and why our soul—and the souls of those we love—lives eternally. I felt as if I were remembering my own experiences as he shared the research in that book. I would take quick gasps and say "oh my gosh, I remember this" as I read the stories. If you are interested in broadening your vision of new thought, don't miss picking up this book and diving in. It is a fascinating journey.

In my near-death experience, I was given another opportunity to see beyond the typical view of the human mind. While attending the Avatar course, I had a mystical experience of what that original separation must have felt like. And, believe me, I didn't like that feeling! However, it gave me some wonderful insights that, again, changed my life for the better. During an exercise that assisted me in getting my ego-mind out of the way, which enabled me to connect to my higher self or, as some people call it, the higher consciousness or God self, I experienced a vivid and disturbing sensation of leaving (falling away from) what I perceived as "the fold" of love. God itself. While I was in that "fold," it felt very similar to the sensations that I had in my near-death experience when the robed beings flooded me with a beautiful energy of love. Then, abruptly, I was being catapulted out of that beauty and grace, far away from the warmth of compassion and security of unconditional love. What followed was a sensation of deep loss and a profound sense of sadness to have left that source, the Creator/God. (I even cried, and, at that time, I rarely cried.) I believe that it was through having this experience that I truly began to understand the desire that I had to get back to what felt like home: back home into that sensation of intense unconditional love and togetherness.

I also sense now that I chose to leave that fold in order to find my way back again, a happier and more evolved and loving being, even when I couldn't see, touch or feel, or have proof that there was a god source that loving. I see that it was part of my life plan (applying the "everything happens for a reason") to create drama after drama and learn the experiential lessons.

I now believe, after having had both the near-death experience and that spiritual "aha" in Avatar (where I once again had the blessing of feeling that indescribable sensation of love), that it shifted me or reminded me of my home. These experiences rebirthed my awareness and shifted my perspective as a whole and lifted the veil for me to know once again my soul's purpose.

Yes, by looking beyond my old habits of tapping into fear and placing judgment on others and myself, I now can embrace this newfound sense of understanding what lies beyond our limited view of the world.

I sense that I knew of this agreement to come back into this "forgetfulness" or darkness or, as some reference it, the lack of spiritual awareness that exists in humanity right now, long before making the decision to come here and play out my part as a teacher/healer in this particular role, on this planet. Many of us, the light workers, already knew that we were coming back to awaken others to this truth.

Remember, we are spiritual beings having a human experience.

To explain my understanding of this even further: As part of the original intention and plan for our planet, a veil was placed here for the Creator to seek itself within and to recreate this "heaven," this home, here and now. No other planet was given free will to seek out this truth within. We, humanity, took on the task of experiencing all of what we now call duality (light and dark) and arriving back home with the essence and knowingness that LOVE is all there is.

Victim consciousness was created to transcend and transmute itself back into its pure self by allowing the seeker to experience compassion, forgiveness, peace, joy, humility, tranquillity, non-judgment, and eternal bliss, as a result of knowing the opposites. The darkness is giving birth to the light again through each of us. It is the triumph of that eternal LOVE that is about to change victim consciousness into a pure and loving consciousness for anyone who so chooses.

What is it that we all have spent so many lifetime experiences seeking? The dedication of Our Spirit, on behalf of all humanity, along with our guides and angels, embodies the answer to this question. We are all working in unity. We are spiritual beings having a human experience and we are here to teach others the freedom that understanding this brings them. And, if we are willing, we will receive more answers about these ancient questions as we expand and grow into the oneness again. Taking time to meditate, study, learn, and pray helps us to find answers and our own power within ourselves.

Access Your New Tools and Embrace Their Gifts

You can access many tools to expedite this process of returning to the source of the expansive love from which you came. Your greatest tool is your ability to focus on the intention to receive the gifts of those who have traveled the path before you. Countless books have been and are currently being written prophesying the growing presence of human angels in our lives. They are arriving with ever-increasing frequency. These "human angels," too, will guide you to your own eternal experience of oneness, if you consciously choose to awaken, listen, and act on their guidance. Choose to be open and receptive, and intend not to dwell in negativity, darkness, and judgment; that will benefit your soul greatly as these times of change descend on this planet. Surround yourself with the pure light of the Creator and *be* that light. You will continually increase the feeling of being safe and loved at all times if you do this. You will also grow to understand that it is always a wise choice to react out of love and not fear and grow to be aware of the difference more and more clearly as you practice accepting more love and light into your life. I sure have.

I have loved exploring new ideas and concepts during the past ten years. I even read books that had been left out of the Bible I grew up with. All of this research helped me to process what I'd been indoctrinated to believe by my church and family, take it one step further, and decide what I believed based on information I hadn't been exposed to in my early years. I began to come into my own and my passion to come to terms with my own personal concept of God grew stronger as my studies continued. I felt more of a sense of a personal relationship to God than I ever had before and I enjoyed that very much! Through this processing, I also felt a sense of trust and self-confidence in my own reasoning, which was growing inside me. The healing I did through this inward searching began to reflect in my outward life. I was drawn to others who were like-minded about individuality and honoring each other's beliefs. My new personal beliefs entailed less and less desire to find answers from others and more of the drive to keep going within for answers.

I suggest that you simply silence yourself, even for only a few minutes at a time, to check *within* for a sensation of peace (you practice getting in tune with your intuition this way); for therein lies your own personal awareness, an awareness of your truth as you are exposed to the teachings to which your own soul guides you. I certainly tapped into that peace and have experienced some amazing miracles over the past few years. When you meditate, ask for God, your guardian angels, or guides to help you. Just use discernment as you study these materials and then choose to accept the emanating and overpowering sense of LOVE you will experience as a result of being in their presence. I have grown to believe (and from firsthand experience, I might add) that we all have around us guides and angels who are more than willing to help. Going within and trusting your discernment through your feelings creates a personal sense of knowing and calmness about these encounters. Buddha really got this point across well when he said: Believe nothing just because a so-called wise person said it. Believe nothing just because a belief is generally held. Believe nothing just because it is said in ancient books. Believe nothing just because it is said to be of divine origin. Believe nothing just because someone else believes it. Believe only what you yourself test and judge to be true.

Understand and be aware on your search that authentic teachers never project fear-based prophecies. They never teach in any way that causes us to fear a negative outcome for not accepting their assistance or for not believing things they tell us to believe. A good teacher will never tell us that their way is the only way. They will never judge us for choosing a different path. We are to discover our own "salvation"—within.

Truth Is What Brings You Joy and Truth Is What Sets You Free

I also found that there was a whole lot of joy in finding my own truth, my own salvation, if I may. And with that joy, a sensation of empowerment. I also began to reason through my studies that the mass consciousness of humanity has been preparing for this shift in consciousness for some time now. It is obvious, just by seeing how American society alone has opened up to honoring diversity in its population, that we all had to learn to honor our diverse religious preferences in order to live side by side in peace. Really, we didn't have a choice. And although there are portions of our population that do not like this change at all, there was no way to stop it from happening. Love is one powerful force that just can't be stopped in its tracks. I also feel that the acceptance by so many of angelic presence in their lives was part of the common ground that helped make the transition itself somewhat more acceptable.

5
Angels among Us

Come to the edge! Life said
"We are afraid" They said
Come to the edge! Life said
They came
It pushed them
And they flew...

—Guillaume Appollinaire

Yes, I Do Believe That the Angels Are among Us

I'm not embarrassed to talk about my belief in Angels. I never was. I guess that it wasn't taboo to talk about angels in my Baptist upbringing. And so, I felt free to share the one part of my "gift of out-of- the-ordinary perceptions" of these "other worldly spirits." I freely spoke of my awareness of angels, and still do today.

Due to this fact, I often heard fascinating stories from acquaintances and friends —of their own experiences with angels —especially Guardian Angels. One of my best friends shared an amazing story of a first hand experience with an Angel, and I'd like to share it here.

It went like this. She and her daughter were walking out of a grocery store one day. Her daughter was four years old and a somewhat more reserved and quiet child than most.

As they were heading toward their car, she startled my friend by stating "Mommy, look at that angel!" A bit confused, my friend asked her daughter what she meant. Her daughter went on to describe a b-e-a-u-t-i-ful angel and told her that "She" was right behind a young employee that was standing outside having a cigarette on his break to the right of the stores exit, pointing right in his direction.

My friend listened to her child describe how pretty the angel was and politely acknowledged to her daughter that she had heard what she had explained to her and headed home shortly thereafter.

The little girls' grandmother worked at that same grocery store, and so my friend decided to tell her that story the next day. The grandmother looked rather surprised as she told her the details about the experience. When my friend finished the story, the grandmother went on to tell my friend that that same young man had been in a life-threatening car accident the night before and had miraculously survived —after being covered in gasoline and not discovered for several hours after the accident had occurred.

Needless to say, my friend was stunned by this news and most certainly didn't think that it was a coincidence!

I've heard (and read about) many stories about strange happenings related to "guardian angel-type stories" since then, yet I will never forget that particular story.

Songs such as "Angels Among Us" made popular by the country band, Alabama, have always touched my heart. If you haven't heard of that one, I'd suggest looking up the lyrics on the Internet, for a heart-warming tale of an angel.

Another favorite song of mine was by the rock band Train, titled "Calling All Angels." Look the lyrics up on the Internet or buy the album "Alive at Last." It really is a wonderful song that begins with

"I need a sign to let me know you're here. All of these lines being crossed over the atmosphere. I need to know that things are gonna look up, 'cause I feel us drowning in a sea spilled from a cup."

When I discovered that people of all faiths believe in angels, it didn't take long for me to realize that it wasn't very logical for people who grew up on the other side of the planet in a completely different culture to have to believe exactly the way that I did and, furthermore, that God would condemn them to some forsaken hell for believing in the religion their parents taught them. Those were some very important beliefs for me to release while sorting out my own spirituality.

I had already concluded that angels are with everyone. It is widely accepted that we are all assigned a guardian angel. And it doesn't seem to matter to those guardian angels what religion, if any, we choose to be, as they love us unconditionally. If they are indeed messengers of God, I choose to believe that they are all working with the same universal God.

Adding a Dose of "Common Sense"

A large dose of good old common sense came into my thought process when I was able to widen my view and let go of the limiting thinking that my way was the only right way. As I mentioned earlier, communication in our world has been opened up globally through the Internet and I found that some wonderfully kind, loving, Godlike beings *do* live outside the United States and haven't been raised in Christian doctrine. I have truly enjoyed connecting with them! If I were writing an e-mail right now, I'd place the LOL (it means "Laugh Out Loud") here!

Yep, and pardon the slang, but I am getting down home and here with you, I really do believe that this is a time of great change and that millions of people are being prepared for this change in the days to come. I also see that, with a little help from our friends on the "other side of the veil," we are being given hope when we need it most. All of the writings and doctrines that I have been led to are simply "God in action."

Of course, you can always "Google" the word "angels" and there will be *43,400,000* URLs for *angels!* Now that bit of information, in and of itself, would spark an interest for me in finding out a lot more about our "feathered friends."

6
Helpful Breathing Exercises

Homage to the Breath
Breathing In, Breathing Out, Breathing In, Breathing Out
Like a wave the breath arises from and dissolves back into the
    source,
Guiding us into the Stillness, We remember who we are
Radiant, luminous, eternal, energy
Arising at birth, Dissolving at death
Back into the Source.
                      —*Stephanie Kristal, M.A., R.Y.T.*

We are birthed into this world on the in breath and released from this world on the out breath. As long as we live, the breath *breathes* our body, creating a beautiful dance of expansion and contraction. Yet we pay little attention to this miracle—this gift of life.

I've found on my journey away from the victim mindset that deep-breathing tools are incredibly powerful. Generally, the purpose of deep-breathing meditation is to calm the mind and develop inner peace.

Many good books and audios in the marketplace teach about

the positive effects of deep-breathing exercises. Yoga, which emphasizes deep breathing, has become very popular in our society.

For the longest time, I found myself reading self-help and spiritual healing books and stories. I would rarely take the time to do the exercises, however. I began to understand my spirituality from the intellectual standpoint, but I was not feeling the changes in my life on a deeper level. It is one thing to "know in our heads" what to do in our lives, and quite another to know in our bodies. "Word experiences" are easy. But when I quit ignoring the exercises in healing books and began to practice them, my healing process accelerated tremendously. I had often read about the importance and value of using breathing techniques during my studies, and also had heard firsthand about the effectiveness from various other light workers during our conversations, and therefore decided to give it a try. I was amazed at how quickly I could relax myself and find serenity in such a short period of time when I started to use breathing techniques. I encourage you to practice these exercises—and do so daily.

The Definition of Divinity

I use the word "divinity" in my exercises and Merriam-Webster's online dictionary describes "divinity" as "the quality or state of being divine." And "divine" as "of, relating to, or proceeding directly from God or a god." As you know, I believe that God is love. We all have various meanings attached to the word "love" and so I reference this particular part of the description from Merriam-Webster's online dictionary as well, because it describes what I interpret love to be in my own daily life so eloquently.

Center Yourself

Center yourself and focus on receiving the gifts before you. Life is full of gifts; we just need to unwrap them! We can release the old chains of despair and victimhood, and embrace the gift of truth with ease. You can begin to manifest a beautiful reality.

Simply affirm that you will choose to manifest only what is for your Divine will when you enter your meditation time with your breathing exercises.

If you'd like, you can imagine yourself surrounded with a beautiful white healing light coming down through the top of your head, moving down into your body with ease. Get comfortable in your favorite chair or in the traditional lotus (legs crossed in front of you, arms resting on your knees, with your hands facing up) position. Be sure to take deep breaths in up from the abdomen. I also suggest that you breathe in slowly through your nose and blow out through your mouth.

Let's Start the Exercise

Now, breathe in your divinity. Own it. Ask your angels, those messengers who have been working so hard for you, to continue to expand your capacity to hold the higher vibrations of the love.

The Breath of Life is in unity. We are all One.

Do this with me now. Simply close your eyes, relax, and take a deep breath:

Breathe it in—receive.
Breathe it out—give it back.

It is so simple. . . . Feel the beautiful essence of Divinity.

Practice this mantra at any time throughout your day. There is no need to close your eyes every time you do this. Taking long, deep breaths can calm you down at any moment. Just envision the peace flooding in. This will calm you, relax you, and put you into your center. Breathe in deeply through your nose and breathe out through your mouth. I used to breathe in the sensation of the beautiful countryside on my drives up to visit my family and friends. I had moved a half an hour away from them and this gave me a great opportunity to spend some time relaxing and using this exercise. I'd breathe the beauty, in gratitude, and on my out-breath I would release any tension that I'd been feeling that day. It really was so relaxing, and the peaceful attitude of gratitude that I would experience while doing that exercise was uplifting to my emotions for the rest of the day.

Breathe it in—receive.
Breathe it out—give it back.

The Circle of Life now transcends death. Expansion.

Breathe it in—receive.
Breathe it out—give it back.

Healing made effortless in this moment. Focus on the "effortless" as you breathe with this one.

Breathe it in—receive.
Breathe it out—give it back.

No need for you to fear . . . continue to expand to the higher vibrations of love.
Now, release the fears on your out-breath, as you do this breathing exercise.

Breathe it in—receive peace.
Breathe it out—release the fears to your angels. Give it back.

Receive your divinity. Feel the peace, joy, harmony, and bliss of your God-self as you breathe this time. Imagine a beautiful deep-blue color when breathing in.

Breathe it in—receive.
Breathe it out—give it back . . . flood those around you with this peace, joy, and bliss.

Share this feeling with all around you.

Own your divinity. Now, meditate on accepting your empowerment as you breathe in, and acknowledge that it is for the highest good of all, while you now accept and own your Divinity as you breathe out.

Breathe it in—receive.
Breathe it out—give it back.

Repeat this practice regularly, for this is especially powerful in your healing process!

Breathe it in—receive.
Breathe it out—give it back.

Get to know your divinity. Now, focus on feeling your divinity on all levels—body, mind, and spirit—as you breathe in the joy, peace, and endless source of love of the Divine.

Breathe it in—receive.
Breathe it out—give it back.

Feel your divinity. Feel the freedom of choosing the beauty and power of peaceful living as you breathe in. And now, breathe out the negative judgments. Let them go and give them to the creator to transmute them back into unconditional love.

Breathe it in—receive.
Breathe it out—give it back.

And, so it is.

Practice these exercises as often as possible, preferably daily . . . and experience the expansion in your capacity to "BE" LOVE NOW.

7

The Healing Power of Music, Dance, and Exercise

Whatever the Mind of Man can Conceive and Believe it can Achieve.

—*Andrew Carnegie*

**Make Your Own Kind of Music,
Sing Your Own Kind of Song**

I am a firm believer in the power of music and its healing faculties. Revisiting some of our more happy childhood experiences often can give us some ideas for bringing back happiness into our adult life. For instance, I remember as a child, even on days when I was bored or lonely, when I would go outside and start singing some of my favorite songs at the top of my lungs to my dog, Sam. (By the way, we lived out in the country.) I'd even sit on the top of his doghouse, or swing on the swing nearby, as I burst out into song, and he'd often sing along with his howl. It may sound silly, but it was such fun! On days when I felt sad or lonely, doing this routine just seemed to erase my sadness and bring up some very happy and joyful feelings. Whether it was an old Helen Reddy song, with lyrics that I would belt out like, "Keep on singing, don't stop singin' you're gonna be a star someday," or imitating Karen Carpenter using a hairbrush as a microphone in front of the living room window or mirror and singing, "I'm on the top of the world," while imagining myself on a stage in front of thousands of people, it generated a lot of good mood feelings.

Again, I can giggle at this notion now, but I can tell you with a smile on my face that remembering that time brings a sense of happiness and warmth to my soul. Back then, I would let myself envision or dream, and I'd pretend that it was really happening. I became the star of that moment. And, at that moment, I didn't have another care in the world. Obviously, pop music has changed since the 1970s, but I still saw my own teenage daughter do the same things just a few years back. Music is so uplifting and many a musician will tell you that music has saved their lives. It gave them an outlet for their energies and gave them focus to work hard at becoming good at something when nothing else may have interested them. I've heard plenty of people talk about how music can spontaneously transport them to another place and time. A certain song comes on the radio and it instantly reminds them of a childhood event or that special love from years gone by. Of course, an old love song can bring up sadness as well, but our goal in this book is to be persistent with using tools that raise our vibrations and guide us to more happiness and contentment.

> **Nothing great was ever achieved without enthusiasm.**
> —*Ralph Waldo Emerson*

Kids of all ages love listening to their favorite music stars at live concerts. Or they may choose to watch their favorite artists get creative with their videos on the television. Music is a common ground for people of every background to celebrate the good things about life.

Have a Good Cry to a Sad Song

Allowing yourself to feel all of your feelings is very important. You don't want to be stuffing them down anymore. It is too hard on your physical body. The body's immune system runs overtime and gets worn down from too much mental stress. This is why I highly recommend using music to help heal, as it is one powerful medium. There are ample love songs, songs about angels, songs about good times, and songs about the not-so-happy times out there. In fact, if you need a good cry for a little release, well then, put on a sad song and let it go. Take some private time and give yourself five or ten minutes, or 15, for that matter (it is good to put a sensible time limit on it, though), to just let the tears flow (guys, you can do this too!) and you'll be amazed at how much better you can feel. This would be a great time to "flip switch," as Lynn Grabhorn taught in *The* Excuse Me, Your Life Is Waiting *Playbook*. She taught an exercise in this workbook: You 1) purposely think of a sad event from your life (she had you write it down); 2) let yourself feel that feeling that comes up; and 3) stop after a minute or two and "flip the switch" (the emotion) to focus on some experience or event that immediately brings happy feelings to your heart and mind. And a happy song could instantly do this. Be inventive with your healing process and, again, have fun with it!

You really can learn how to control your emotions by practicing these types of exercises and then you can become quite skilled at choosing how you want to express your feelings. You decide whether you want to change your thoughts to something more positive. It's really pretty simple. It's very empowering to do this, as you can become less and less involved with letting your emotions run your moods. You learn to be in control of the moment and that is a remarkable feeling! Other people can't pull you out of your center so easily and that, too, can be worth its weight in gold.

Music Lifts Your Spirits

If you just want to stay upbeat and keep the momentum going, take some time out to find some upbeat music on the radio or Internet, or dig out that favorite old album, tape, or CD. Let yourself rock out, veg out, or be soothed by some relaxing music. Join a local choir, or make a singing group or band of your own for the fun of it. Use music to lift your mood, make your spirit soar, and stay in the happy zone for as long as you can. So many of us have forgotten about the simple joys in life and need to be reminded.

There are many wonderful healing CDs out on the market and even more beautiful songs filled with lyrics about good times and celebration. Apply persistence on this healing journey, fan the flame of happiness whenever you think about it, and remember you are the victor, not the victim.

Dance

I've also had fun with my daughter and some of my friends by just letting loose and dancing in my own living room. We danced and just let it all go and had a blast. I have also turned on the tunes when I was alone and just danced. Nobody was there to judge how I was dancing and it gave me such a sense of freedom and joy. The exercise alone raised the "feel good" chemicals in my brain (endorphins) and brought me into a more pleasant emotional state.

You could also sign up at a local dance studio for classes or if the funds aren't available, go to the library and rent a "how to" video and learn some new dance moves. It can make you feel years younger and the "footloose and fancy free" sensation that you get lifts your mood many notches. Not to mention, expanding your world to include music through learning a new dance makes you feel like you've accomplished something special just for yourself. It's important to stretch yourself a little and try new things as you let go of the old.

Exercise

Exercise plays an important role in releasing stress and raising levels of our natural endorphins, which are chemicals in our brain that lift our mood and reduce our stress levels. Exercise has plenty of benefits for our body, such as flushing out toxins and improving our overall health. The exercise doesn't have to be intense; you can simply go outside and take a walk or play a non-competitive game of tennis for fun. Getting outside when weather permits has the added benefit of getting out into nature and lifting your mood. There are also thousands of exercise videos, including dancing, kickboxing, yoga, aerobics, and various toning types that will give you a variety of workouts to get your body in shape and lift your mood. I found that having a friend or acquaintance participate with me often gave me the extra push that I needed on days when I might have put it off. It also is a great idea to get your children (if you have them) away from the television and into a family routine of exercise. If you can't afford to join a health club, there are walking clubs at local malls and gymnasiums at various public schools that offer free or very inexpensive access to various workout activities indoors.

8
Being Present

The present moment holds infinite riches beyond your wildest dreams but you will only enjoy them to the extent of your faith and love. The more a soul loves, the more it longs, the more it hopes, the more it finds. The will of God is manifest in each moment, an immense ocean that only the heart fathoms insofar as it overflows with faith, trust, and love.
—*Jean-Pierre De Caussade,* The Sacrament of the Present Moment

When in Minnesota, I often visit one of the largest bulk herb and homeopathic remedy retail stores in the country. That store is called Present Moment. I always had thought it was a very clever name, but once I really came to understand the importance of doing just that, living in the present moment—I grew very fond of that name.

The Basic Practice

Being present in the spiritual sense always has a double meaning. There's present, as in being here, in attendance. And there's present, as in now, a moment of time. What is the spiritual practice of being present? Being here now.

The world's religions all recommend living in the moment with full awareness. Zen Buddhism, especially, is known for its emphasis on "nowness." Hindu, Taoist, Jewish, Moslem, Christian, and other teachers urge us to make the most of every day as an opportunity that will not come to us again. Now, of course, we are living in the present moment. Where, or more to the point, *when* else would we be living? Frankly, in truth, many of us live every*where* (or every*when*) except the present moment! As victims, we tended to spend a lot of time dwelling or concentrating on the past and/or worrying about the future. That is because so often we were feeling quite uncomfortable with the chaotic lifestyles that we had created from not thinking about our "future selves" when making decisions in the "now." Do I have you confused yet? What I am getting at here is if we all will learn to love and accept ourselves regardless of the past (without judgment), we can rest in our everyday moments with peace and contentment. We really can learn to enjoy life! If we keep beating ourselves up for past decisions that may have caused us pain or unhappiness, what good does that do anyway? You can't change the past. It's over. What you can do is apply self-forgiveness and let that old baggage go. You can handle *anything* if you just stay in the now. It's only the fears and worries sneaking up on you through your emotions that cause the discomfort; and you are learning in this book not to be a victim to anything, including your emotions.

This concept of the present moment is sometimes referred to as "mindfulness" in Eastern religions. It actually originated as a Buddhist concept, but it is now incorporated into many stress management programs, and for a good reason. If we live our lives mindfully, we will get more out of life.

What This Practice Does

Really, living in the present moment is about having a complete awareness and appreciation of the life we have, right here and right now. By doing what you are doing right now in *this* present moment, taking time to realize what is really important in

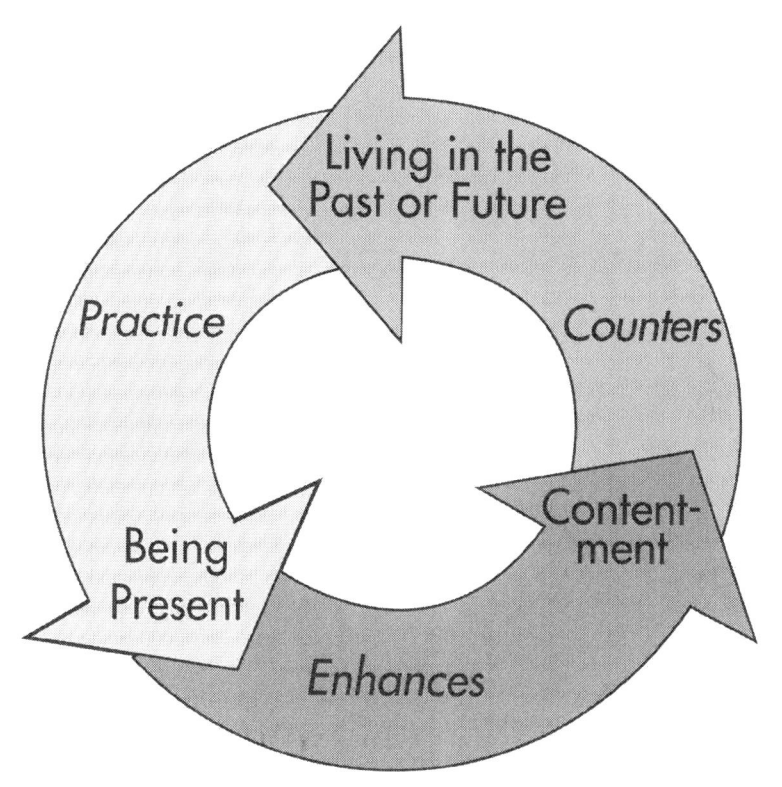

Figure 8-1.

your life by spending time in self-exploration and study, you can come to find a sense of safety and peace. That peace has always been within you and, underneath all of the turmoil that you may have created in your life when living in the victim mindset, all you really need to learn to do is to surrender to a belief that you can choose at any time to "just say no" to that mind chatter. The breathing exercises in chapter 6 are wonderful at helping you to do that. Simply taking a moment to do nothing but pay attention to your in-breath and out-breath promptly refocuses your energy into a peaceful state anytime and anywhere.

Get rid of all of your emotional baggage, calm your worries about the future, and start enjoying the peace and happiness that can only be found in the present moment.

Through a little more introspection in your spiritual journey, you can also find out what are the true causes of stress in your life. Often something as simple as the lack of forgiveness and the habit of judging yourself and others can cause you to feel stressed and uncomfortable. By increasing your awareness of your inner self and using (practicing) the tools I teach in this book, you can transform that old victim mindset from focusing on stress and discontentment to no longer letting your emotions rule you. In fact, you can learn to let those emotions guide and teach you more about your true self.

The Benefits of Being Mindful Are Bountiful

Once you master the technique of centering yourself and are able to be more comfortable just "being," rather than always "doing" something, you then can become a more carefree and happy person in each and every "present moment." Being present is a far better choice than needing to go into the past or out into the future with the "someday" and "if only's," which most definitely put the present moment out there somewhere in the could-have-been and should-have-been zones.

Eckhart Tolle had a best-selling book in the United States entitled *The Power of Now*. I garnered a tremendous amount of wisdom from his book and began to see that by practicing living in the now, the present moment in time, I was able to find far greater peace in my life overall. When I wasn't busy worrying about the future or blaming my miseries on the past, I found that I could empower myself to appreciate each day as it came. In the book *When Things Fall Apart*, Pema Chödrön wrote beautifully about the now, the present moment. Here is an excerpt from this book: "Now is the only time. How we relate to it creates the future. In other words, if we're going to be more cheerful in the future, it's because of our aspiration and exertion to be cheerful in the present. What we do accumulates; the future is the result of what we do right now."

9

Leaving Fear Behind

> Courage is resistance to fear, mastery of fear, not absence of fear.
> —*Mark Twain*

"What about fear?" you might ask. To be afraid or apprehensive of something is an unpleasant experience, to say the least. Fear can and will steal your power if you let it. Fear is a strong emotion that can cripple you and rob you of your peace. But it also serves a good purpose by causing us to anticipate or be aware of danger. When allowed to get out of control, however, those emotions can cause us to make some poor decisions. Often, an uncomfortable feeling in the form of an emotional uneasiness (what many of us recognize as a "gut instinct") is simply your intuition warning you to "be aware" of pending or potential danger. Practice paying attention to your body and emotions more often, rather than ignoring them, and you will grow to become better and better at dealing with whatever life experiences come your way. Really, everything has a purpose, even fear, but I encourage you to remember one of Franklin Roosevelt's most famous quotes: "The only thing we have to fear is fear itself."

Again, when you learn to be the observer in your life, and get into the habit of reminding yourself that you are "a spiritual being having the human experience," you will be able to quickly disengage yourself from letting fear take hold of your decision-making process. You will be able to call forth the courage that you have *within* yourself to handle anything that comes your way. Staying in the present moment is a remarkable way to do this. Fear most often comes from memories of painful past experiences and creates worry about future experiences. Taking a deep breath and staying in the present moment immediately disengages fear.

There is no need to fear failure. A lesson will keep returning, repeating itself, until we understand, heal, and own our responsibility for it. Remember: Once a lesson is healed, it's healed! Done! Own that power and feel the new sense of freedom that you have. How wonderful and freeing this can be. Moving forward by releasing the fear, anger, and other negative emotions while you embrace the light and freedom releasing brings is a huge step in shedding victim consciousness. It has worked in my own life and it will in yours, too, if you choose to apply this wisdom.

Let me give you one more example. If you cut yourself, that wound is very sensitive until you start healing. In fact, a little bump or bit of pressure on that wound can cause a great deal of pain. However, when given some time to heal, the wound becomes less sensitive and by the time it is completely healed, the same pressure that would have sent you into discomfort and/or a lot of pain is no longer noticeable at all. The body's remarkable ability to heal itself is a great example, because, you see, the same goes for your emotional healing capabilities. Your emotional healing will cause you to become less sensitive to criticism, reduce episodes of fear getting out of control, and receive other wonderful gifts.

10

Learning to Create Your New Life

We cannot do great things on this earth. We can only do small things with great love.

—*Mother Teresa*

As we move into a more comfortable space of being at peace with our own spiritual belief systems, and hence gaining clarity about who we are and what our life purpose on this planet is, you most certainly will realize that victimhood is not something you wish to "wear" anymore. We can began to take control of our lives; it becomes much easier, and you can learn to intentionally manifest (deliberately create something) or, as I put it here, co-create with God. You see, by

- taking the step or action of owning your divinity,
- focusing on living *(and loving yourself)* in the present moment,
- and taking responsibility for your life and decisions,

you are given the opportunity to make choices from a higher or clearer space. We really can see where it is that we want to go and what it is that we truly want to do with our lives. It is so much more joyful to live life by deliberately taking action rather than by constantly having to be on the defensive or in reaction mode. It can be something as simple as choosing love over fear, and it then becomes co-creating a more pleasant experience in that moment. Co-creating with God isn't always about manifesting *things,* it is about manifesting the peace of mind, contentment, and satisfaction of just being who you are in that moment. Don't forget to appreciate yourself and all of the hard work that you are doing. Take time to be grateful for yourself.

Doing so also gives you the foundation for setting realistic goals, as sensible, well-thought-out goals align with our higher purpose. These types of focused goals rarely have resistance. In fact, your life begins to "go with the flow" rather than seeming like you are always swimming upstream. When your life begins to "flow" and you become more confident in your abilities to chart your own course in life, you can practice staying focused and you aren't at the whim of others, nor do you let your own out-of-control and sometimes erratic emotions run the show like they used to. You create your life with a positive mindset, and in doing so, you are co-creating with God, as God, in the simplest way possible. By becoming synchronized with the vision of your higher self or God self, you own your divinity; you automatically connect with the ability to create effortlessly. Through your "in breath," you receive knowledge and clarity. Through your "out breath," you give it back and create the life you want to live. (Check out Author's Insight 11, "Create Your Divinity," in the back of this book, and revisit it often.)

Other Resources

There are also plenty of great books available on manifesting. One of my very favorites is *Excuse Me, Your Life Is Waiting*, by Lynn Grabhorn. (I just can't seem to recommend this book enough!)

You can also learn how to manifest your desires with the book

Ask and It Is Given, from Esther and Jerry Hicks, explaining how the Abraham teachings work and offering 22 powerful processes for putting them into practice. Check it out at www.abraham-hicks.com.

Once you step off the victim treadmill you will have a blast creating a whole new life for yourself. Let's keep going here and *get real* about the next steps in your healing process.

11

Getting Real

A man is about as happy as he makes his mind up to be.
—Abraham Lincoln

A Challenging Journey

As most of you know, living on this planet presently is "intense." Living in the victim consciousness is full of extremes—drama and pain, peaks and valleys of emotion. The journey is challenging and at times overwhelming. I'm getting real here. Although I am experiencing much more peace and joy in my life, there are still moments when I feel like throwing in the towel. I still have moments when I get overwhelmed by life. I momentarily lose faith that I can maintain this new way of living for the long haul. This process of healing is not for weaklings. I believe that if you were led to this book, you are strong and capable of succeeding beyond your wildest dreams. You have what it takes to free yourself of old habits, beliefs, and patterns.

Think about this carefully: No more energy or effort is required to aim high in life—to create happiness, abundance, and health from life—than is required to accept misery, poverty, and emotional pain.

I am happy to report that those moments of feeling overwhelmed no longer last for long periods of time. Just as I still do, remind yourself of the message above, often. Repetition is the oldest way of learning. The ancient Greeks learned by imitating great masters—teachers who had their students do the same exercises over and over again. We know that it takes repetition to create new habits. I strongly encourage each of you to spend time with the insights and exercises in the next chapter. Spend time meditating on at least one of the insights throughout the day. If you choose, visit my website (www.avictimnomore.com), where I offer a special section to help you with this. Simply go to the "Insight of the Day" button, and click on an insight. You will be given an affirmation to repeat throughout the day.

If you want to change your life, to live free of the victim consciousness, and you expect your life to change overnight, hang on to that passionate expectation—please just know that it's going to take some time, time well spent. Be willing to work not only hard, but smart. Working smart is applying this new knowledge in your life. Working hard is simply about applying your determination to the process. It's about practice. In essence, you are going to learn some spiritual practices here. You will practice living from your authentic self, your higher self. I've heard "spiritual practice" described as an action that prepares us to overcome difficulties. Never succumb to adverse circumstances.

You may very well be on the verge of changing the course of your life entirely by applying this spiritual practice! To get real, you will need to keep working to release the old ways. Work toward replacing negative beliefs and patterns with new habits and positivism. You will surely see progress occurring in your life if you stick to it. Joy will begin to replace the old misery. Of this I am sure. The ups and downs will no longer be as dramatic and emotionally draining as in the past. I am living proof of that. When you finish reading this book, there will be no shortage of tools for you to use in creating your successful new life.

We've learned some great insights and ideas thus far in this book as to what it takes to overcome our old patterns of playing the role of the victim. Now it's up to us to use those insights and imitate the masters by applying that wisdom in our daily lives. This book provides you with a set of tools, insights, and exercises to use over and over again. Apply these practices in the same way a karate student prepares to attain a black belt: with repetition. Together, we are seeking to become "black belts in living free of the victim consciousness."

No Way but Up

I've come to realize that there is a deep truth to the motto "We are never given more than we can handle." The fact that I am here now, sharing this book with you, is living proof of this. I've learned that we can never go back to the lower levels of the healing process once we've healed, released, and replaced the confusion and pain with love and light. Believe it!

I encourage you to make a promise to yourself on this journey that you will continue to be willing. No matter how frustrating this journey may be at times, be willing to keep moving forward. That is the first step. Keep this promise close to your heart, and you will never lose your faith and hope.

During my upbringing, I was often told by my mother that we are never given more than we can handle (a positive indoctrinated belief for me). This is one belief that I like to hang on to when times have gotten a bit rough. Positive beliefs that include this type of wisdom are important for us to draw on when we get discouraged. Personally, I still have "issues" and areas to heal. By being willing to put forth the effort and by working hard to incorporate these teachings into my own life, I continue to realize positive results. I continue to draw uplifting people into my life. I am stronger and wiser and I am projecting higher vibrations out into the universe. And the people I face each day of my life mirror what I teach—right back at me. This applies to my friendships and to my family. My daughter has become very good at reminding me of what I teach when I temporarily fall back into old patterns! And when she does, it helps. It refocuses my resolve to move forward. Our students truly are our teachers. The more I share my insights and healing tools with others, the more I am equally blessed on my own path with healing and joy from their insights and successes.

I start my day with affirmations such as: "I am worthy," "I will stay out of judgment of myself and others today," and "Expand my ability to love and be loved." I am empowering myself to live free of the victim consciousness. I do my best to work in sync with my higher guidance in this present moment and keep looking forward. I simply keep focusing on my own healing process and I am willing to learn from each situation that arises. That's getting real!

In times of doubt, I discipline myself. I choose to visualize those doubts right smack in the middle of my heart, and I see them transmuted into love and faith. I also choose not to judge myself for minor setbacks. By applying this practice, your heart (your higher self) will become more familiar with working in sync with you. Old patterns will be replaced with new ones. You will begin to see changes in your life in a very positive way! These positive changes will appear in your life experiences and will truly prove that the willingness, effort, desire, determination, and focus of your intentions are an act of true self-love, unconditional love. You are forming a new set of life patterns that will eventually replace the victim lifestyle.

Let's give ourselves credit for making it this far. Let's also commit:

- To quit looking back. The past is just that, the past.

- To remember to stop and rest in the present moment. Pause to go within, breathing in your Divinity. When you do this, you will find that all is well in this moment.

- To hold our intention and put forth effort toward "being" free of victimhood, fully trusting and believing that the results will be incredibly wonderful and freeing!

I still get excited when I take the time to count my blessings. When I do, I see how far I have come. The changes are simply amazing!

We simply need to practice patience with ourselves while mastering this process. Ask the angels to send you signs to keep you encouraged on your path. Then pay attention; they never fail to appear. Getting real is about understanding that it will take practice to apply the tools I am sharing with you and then using them repeatedly until this becomes your new way of confronting issues in your life. I repeat: Like anything in life, you have to practice the same technique over and over again to become good at it. Make a commitment to yourself to do this. Let me give you an example of how I applied this process in my own life.

I had just made a demand to the universe, stating that I wanted to learn, once and for all, about how to change old patterns related to financial abundance. I had already discovered some major insights about those past patterns, and now I was demanding that I get the opportunity to apply them. The old cliché "Be careful of what you ask for, you just might get it" comes to mind, as I write this!

Honoring Our Limits

I was upset and having a conversation with a confidant of mine. I was extremely frustrated by my current financial situation and I was finally admitting that to someone. Practically everyone in my circle of friends was telling me just to go and get a part-time job to cover my basic bills, but I felt too overwhelmed at that moment to do it. It seemed that out of left field (and my mouth) came the realization that I felt like "a wounded bird." A wounded bird? That really surprised me, and I thought to myself, "Did I really say that out loud?" I went on to share with this friend that I was overwhelmed with what was happening to my business, with the perceived "mistakes" I had made, and with the stress of trying to make sense of it all. It was all bearing down on me emotionally. I went on to say that I felt momentarily incapacitated. It had been a long time since I had felt that way and, let me tell you, I did not like it! I wasn't seeking pity in the form of "poor me," but simply feeling frustrated in the moment. I told my friend that although I knew I had healed tremendously and had come a long way on my path, I still had wounds. And these current circumstances were reopening them. Old memories of being homeless and living in poverty were flooding back to me.

As the conversation progressed, I continued speaking from my heart (and was willing to be vulnerable). I admitted that others seemed to think that because of how far I'd come, I should be able just to pick myself up and "get it together," no matter what. It felt like I was expressing my limitations to someone for the first time. The words came pouring out. I suggested that I had emotional limits and didn't feel strong enough to go out and get another job at this time. I rambled on in my frustration, that my plate seemed too full to add anything to it. And, no matter what others thought about it, the reality was that I felt overwhelmed to the point of being emotionally crippled.

At that instant, the sign that I had asked the angels for earlier in the day came to my mind. The words from the foreword to this book began speaking to me. I recalled what Wes Hamilton had written, that "being emotionally crippled by being victimized is a normal reaction." At that moment, I truly understood what Wes meant. Bells and whistles were going off in my head. And, at that moment, I was more relieved than I could ever admit. Me? Emotionally crippled? From my perspective, I sure didn't feel that way 99 percent of the time, but what a relief it was to admit that I could be momentarily emotionally crippled! It was such a relief to be able to admit these feelings, safely. With that insight, I felt the world being lifted off my shoulders. Aha! Once again, personal power through awareness!

"My God," I thought, "I just let the cat out of the bag and admitted that I was still wounded, not to mention that I revealed I wasn't perfect yet." Although I was teaching the lessons and insights that had been given to me, I wasn't living and breathing every single one of them, in every single moment. Yikes! And with that admission came a release of negative self-judgment that I had been holding over my own head. I felt the physical tension in my shoulders release instantly. The result was that I took the time to process those feelings and was able to feel more centered and calm again. I also was able to take action within a week. I picked up that part-time job to meet my financial obligations while I worked on a solid, long-term financial plan.

Some days my life feels like "peaches and cream," all warm and fuzzy with all of that fluffy stuff. More times than not, I have a sense of being in love with who I am, feeling those warm and wonderful feelings that we all want to experience, as if I am bringing heaven here now. On other days, however, it simply feels like hard work. But what is the alternative? Living the way we were, in the thick of the same old day-to-day life of miserable dramas, with little or no hope of reprieve? At the very least, as you commit to the process of living in the light of higher vibrations that come with healing (even on the days you get weary), you begin to realize that you are creating new, positive memories. With those new memories comes the opportunity to know the feeling of bringing "heaven here now."

From London with Love

The following was an e-mail I sent to friends on returning from a trip to England. I share this letter with you so you know that, although you may have moments of despair and emotionally crippling experiences, if you are willing to work to shed the victim consciousness, the majority of your days will make the tough days well worth it.

> Here I am in London, England, and I've had one of the most incredible days of my life! Since I was a child, this place called out to me, and now I understand why. It is indeed a "home," a home I now recognize. Yes, it is a home from

another time, another dimension, and its familiarity could not be denied for a moment today. I wrote of this in my book, and I shared that I had been experiencing spontaneous past-life recollections of this place since childhood. I "knew" that I was to reunite with this aspect of myself on this trip, and I walked around the streets of this wondrous city today, and into St. James Park, with a feeling that I describe as "a slice of heaven." In fact, I must have said "I am in heaven" dozens of times today. I kept thinking over and over that I had indeed manifested heaven here on earth. It can be done, and the more I experience it, the more real and effortless it becomes to create more of this experience. Heaven here on earth, right here and right now.

I felt as if I were floating on air. The love for everyone and everything flowed out of me effortlessly, as did my ability to soak in the energy I had longed for since childhood. It was a feeling of "being home again." The affirmation that I use almost daily, "to expand my ability to love and be loved, to flow out more of that love," was expressed as naturally and fully as ever as I walked through these streets today, viewing the sites, and even as I sat in the seat of the subway train with a newfound confidence. My fears dissolved. Yes, this truly is another manifestation that has come to pass.

I tell myself that these tools do work! Why am I so surprised by this? I see it day in and day out, and the amazing journey of living what I teach is becoming more and more evident! I am living the mindset of being free of the victim consciousness, and the results are becoming more and more evident each and every day. I know that when the doubts arise and fear comes to the surface, I have set up a team of "supporters" that I safely call upon with my vulnerabilities, and they respond with compassion and love for me that could only be a reflection of the Divinity within myself. The world is a reflection of me. I am growing to understand that statement more every day. I have a safety net set up now, because I fully and unconditionally love myself so deeply. I am thoughtful and conscious about the decision I make in the moment and how it will affect my "future self." What an amazing change in consciousness. What a gift to cherish. Gratitude at its fullest. Confirmations abound when one is in the flow. Moving through and releasing the fear is becoming a new success story in my life—and a testimonial that the tools I teach work!

Let me share with you a bit more about this trip and its obvious lessons to date as I reflect on my very first day spent here.

During the past week in preparation for this trip to England, I was filled with waves of fear. Fear that I wouldn't have enough money for the trip. Fear that I shouldn't take time away from my work in the States. I questioned myself, "Was I falling into old patterns of being irresponsible with my funds out of wanderlust?" Fear that I would not be able to find my way around this foreign country on my own. Fearful memories of a time in Grand Central Station years earlier came surfacing to my mind as I thought about this trip. You see, on a visit to New York City years ago, I had gotten completely turned around in a subway, and panic had set in like never before. On that particular business trip, I had missed my train. Luggage in tow, it was obvious to all that I was not a resident of this city and privy to its ways. At that moment, I realized that I was all alone, very vulnerable, with only two frightful-looking strangers in that dark tunnel. That was my first panic attack.

Despite my considerable experience as a business traveler, I had fallen into this terrible situation and was momentarily paralyzed with fear! And although I made it safely out of that situation that day, those intense feelings of fear returned to me, ever so powerfully, creating a new level of fear far more intense than I could recall ever experiencing before in my travels.

This needed healing. I needed to choose to apply the tool of "focusing on positive thoughts." I needed to remind myself that I was always in control of my response, that I was right where I was supposed to be, and that all was in Divine order at every moment in time. My mind kept going back to that subway and old judgments resurfaced when I remembered that I had been to New York dozens of times before, but still had allowed this to happen.

"Stop!" I reminded myself. These thoughts needed to be replaced with an "I-can-do-it" attitude. No more judgment. What was needed was an attitude that focused my attention on successes and my newfound empowerment, not on past experiences when I lived from the victim consciousness.

The reality is that my intuitive self (a part of myself I was finally beginning to trust) "knew" an angel would show up to assist me with conquering this fear on the trip to England . . . and of course, one did. A woman who sat next to me on the airplane began speaking to me right before we landed, and she decided to "adopt" me and make sure that I got my luggage, purchased the correct ticket, had a good map of the train lines in hand, made it onto the correct train, and was assured of safely making it to my hotel. She didn't leave my side from the moment we got off the plane until we were on the subway and she was assured that I could understand how to read the signs on that train and knew exactly where I would get off. She even stayed on that train longer than she needed to, to be assured that I was comfortable with making the rest of the trip into London by myself. Yes, my friends, there are angels among us. Expect to see them and they will arrive!

More fear-based thinking was surfacing, as well, when I contemplated the fact that this was my first flight since that fateful day back on September 11, 2001. I had attended my cousin's funeral in Seattle and was scheduled to leave for Minnesota on the morning of September 11. I would have been in the air at the very moment that the hijacked planes were flown into the Twin Towers, but the afternoon before, something inside me said, "Go home today, leave this evening." That voice was so strong that I just had to listen to it, and I took a flight home that evening. That was yet another sign that I needed to learn to trust that intuitive voice inside me. It was another confirmation that it was always aligned with my highest good! Funny, I had no fear of terrorism affecting me today as I sat in that airplane seat on my way across the ocean. I felt completely at home and safe as I was once again up in the air, flying like I had loved to do for my entire adult life.

Healing over ambition . . . I ponder this. I seek balance in the process. I fall in love with myself more and more deeply as I process and practice this insight. My burning desire to be God-like is unveiling itself with a new sense of empowerment and expansion, daily.

The next day, I experienced yet another confirmation of trusting in my Divinity, with the assistance of my intuitive self. My attendance at a workshop that was sold out manifested. Even after the e-mail arrived stating that I would not be able to attend, I felt no doubt, none at all, that I would be sitting in that group of people listening and learning from a mentor. I had an appointment and this knowingness could not be shaken. All the time I had "known" I would attend this workshop with Doreen Virtue, that it was part of my path to the next level of evolution. Here I am, staying across the street from the very place that will hold this workshop tomorrow morning, with me in attendance! The words of a favorite song, Edwin McCain's "I Could Not Ask for More," echo in my mind: "These are the moments, I thank God that I'm alive." Yes, I am truly living a life free of the victim consciousness and, my friend, you can, too.

—*Lori Rekowski, May 2004, London, England*

By getting real, by being realistic, you will find that you will have more and more times of resting in peace, harmony, and bliss—the way I felt when I wrote that e-mail. If you begin to apply the tools shared in this book, you will increase your desire to keep moving forward. You will become a more powerful spiritual being, a "bringer of light."

And in the down times, an increasing desire will arise within you to feel that joy again. Those brief down times may even bring you to your knees, to the point that you send an SOS to the universe. But you will quickly be shown the underlying patterns and habits you need to transform. You will see that the struggle is about a lesson, and that lesson is providing you the gift of taking your healing to the next level. When you call out for help, the answers will come to the surface and into your awareness. Your prayers will be heard! Friends, getting real is a good thing!

12
What's REALLY in It for You?

> I try to live in a spiritual consciousness, which says that who I am is a divine creation of Source that *lives* as a divine creation of Source. When you stay in that awareness, then you create what I call the power of intention. You create the ability to be just like God. We came from love. We came from kindness. We came from joy. We came from perfect abundance. If you see yourself that way, then you'll attract that into your life. If you see yourself needing to have other people love you and care for you or buy your books or whatever, then you'll attract lacks, shortages, and needs into your life, and I don't have any lacks or shortages or needs. If people only knew who or what is with them, in them, beside them all the time, they would never worry about anything.
> —*Wayne Dyer, Ph.D., author of* Your Erroneous Zones
> (*interviewed in* Spirituality & Health, *Nov/Dec 2005*)

I titled this chapter "What's REALLY in It for You?" for a good reason. I think that you'll probably agree with me on this: We have all relied on our excuses to keep living our lives as victims far too long! In fact, I used to actually take pleasure in blaming others for my unhappiness. I didn't have to take responsibility for my own actions. And I appeased others in my life who wanted me to stay the way I was so that they didn't have to look at *themselves*. You know the drill. Those are the people you surround yourself with who tell you "don't rock the boat." And I didn't have to ruffle any feathers or face any of my underlying fears. I could come up with just about every excuse that you can think of to keep things the way they were.

However; something happened to me . . . and it happens to millions and millions of other victims out there. There comes a point when the misery and confusion come crashing in—and we just can't take it one more day. In fact, for me, it was that one moment when I thought I could no longer tolerate being alive that brought me down to my own rock bottom—the suicide attempt. I hit that bottom with a thud and woke up from the nightmare in a hospital bed the day after my near-death experience. Once I got home, I screamed at the top of my lungs that "I WILL NOT BE A VICTIM ANYMORE!" And I meant it. I was going to do whatever it took to find my way out of the hole that I had dug myself. How about you? Are you going to wait until that point in your life comes . . . when you have created more misery and pain then you can possibly handle? Or would you like to *stop the insanity*—right here and right now?

I was lucky; I made it out of that suicide attempt without any physical damage. Others have not been so lucky. I met a woman just a few months ago who has a son in need of 24-hour care from the brain damage that he suffered in a suicide attempt. He can't speak and lost much of his brain functioning.

You know the word *regret* extremely well if you are living in the thick of victimhood. How about joining me in knocking that word right out of your vocabulary once and for all? Say it: I WILL NOT BE A VICTIM ANYMORE! Now, mean it . . . by putting some gusto behind it, some strong feelings, passionate feelings. Muster up everything that you have inside you and say it again: I WILL

NOT BE A VICTIM ANYMORE! I intend to change my life once and for all! Good, there you have it. You've made your commitment. Go find a mirror, look right smack dab into your eyes and now say, "Thank you!" Say it again: "THANK YOU!"

Seriously, speak to yourself in that mirror . . . keep looking deep into your eyes and say:

"I love you!"
"I care about you."
"I think that you are amazing!"
"I am committed to you."
"I can do this!"
"I am not alone; I never was."
"I am that I am."
"I am a magnificent part of all that is."

Now, didn't that feel good? It may feel a little corny, but giggle or laugh out loud at yourself if you must, because practicing this is empowering beyond your wildest dreams.

I can now find a slice of joy in at least something every single day, and the amount of happiness and joy grows stronger and brighter each day that I practice being the "victor." And I am not pulling the wool over your eyes here either. I am still *getting real.*

I learned a long time ago that pretending something is already happening magnetizes that reality to you and that is exactly what has taken place in my life. I pretended the idea of happiness right into my life. I wake up each morning and am thankful that I am alive. Really thankful! I also can now look forward to learning something new every single day of my life. It's like living life through the eyes of a child, with all of the new experiences awaiting me. I pick and choose which experiences I want to create. And those new experiences, sure as heck, are not about new ways to feel pain. No way. I promise you, I really do let joy be part of every day. I even catch myself watching for it.

Joy comes in many forms. For me, it is even in little things like the anticipation of my next phone call with my kids or a friend. I also notice the simplest of things these days. It may be a new way of seeing the beauty in a flower or the variety of birds flying about. Now, rather than being impatient about how long store clerks take to ring up my purchases, I notice that they are actually helping me. In fact, I find great joy in trying to make their day, by looking them in the eye and sincerely asking if they are having a good day. They can tell when someone genuinely cares and I have the neatest experiences doing this. I've even seen how this affects other people in the line behind me. Some have even joined in our conversation and the shopping trip has turned into a special part of my day rather than just an errand.

Have you ever heard that line from the Jack Nicholson movie (*As Good as It Gets*) where he says to Helen Hunt's character, "You make me want to be a better person"? Well, this might sound sappy, but *I* made *myself* want to be a better person.

I notice myself finding beauty in things that I used to look right past in my old dazed way of functioning in the victim mindset. I catch myself looking at the world in a whole new way so often that life feels like a new adventure.

I find gifts showing up each day—like finding a beautiful thought that unexpectedly floats into my consciousness—and I wonder where that warm feeling or little tap on the shoulder just came from. I appreciate those beautiful surprises. I have a sense of connectedness to life that I never used to experience. I also love knowing that I can hear the angels speak to me in this way. I pay special attention to thoughts that just "pop into my head out of nowhere" and embrace the element of surprise that comes from sharing them with others.

Things that I used to take for granted suddenly feel new. They matter, they count! When my daughter phones me now, I actually listen with intent to what she is sharing with me, rather than wondering what I am going to say next. I have the ability to focus on her, rather than on my own problems or thinking my opinion is so important that I interrupt her. What a breath of fresh air for her, too!

Do You Really Want Things to Change?

I know, I know; you can try to excuse yourself and continue to use a whole lot of "if only's," "but's," and "I can't's" . . . but really—there are no "I can't's" . . . just "I won't's"!

I also know deep down inside that if you believe you can, you can. Reach within and pull out that inner strength and power that you've let fall asleep. I think that Anna Quindlen nailed it in her quote: "If your success is not on your own terms, if it looks good to the world but does not feel good in your heart, it is not success at all." You can learn to trust in your ability to find success *on your own terms*. Learn to follow your heart in a practical way. You can do it! As you heal, you learn to master the art of compromise and balance, from within. I have an entire tool chest filled just with action items that you can implement in your life in the next chapter. I dare you . . . dream big and allow yourself to manifest the dream—starting today.

I have seen thousands of people's lives changed. I met them in person at many classes, expos, seminars, and trade shows, and also visited with them online—people who discovered their own inner radar was always there; it just had to be discovered and fine tuned. We all just work on buffing our rough edges and slowly but surely the gem that we are begins to shine ever so brightly.

You don't have to take my word for it. Go ahead; simply surf the websites of the various authors that I mention in this book and you will see testimonials of people just like you, who changed their lives dramatically by applying the same underlying wisdom that I share with you in this book. There are also many forums and chat rooms filled with light workers from all over the world who are doing the same thing that you are—seeking, discovering, and celebrating their newfound inner love, peace, connectedness, and happiness. There are people who have been on this path for ten, 20, 30, even 50 years who can testify to the rewards of living in the understanding that *love is all there is* and that we truly are all interconnected to one another.

Letting Go of Self-Judgment Really Makes a Difference

Okay, this is a biggie! You know as well as I do that critical and demeaning judgment is a projection of fear in one of its many forms. It also is a feeling of "I am right and you are wrong" manifesting itself as a negative opinion that we may say unconsciously. We kick ourselves for making what we perceive as mistakes and beat ourselves up for not living up to someone's (or our own self-imposed) standards. The now famous "What would Jesus do?" motto that was all over the place in the late 1990s was a great one to counter the self-destructive habit of self-righteousness and indignation that comes along with being a judgmental person. I prefer to insert "What would love do?" for my own reminder when I catch myself getting into the judgment mode, whether it is about getting down on myself or someone else.

Personally, I've found that the experience of unconditional love, which has grown to be stronger in my own life, brings with it a whole lot of compassion and acceptance of *all circumstances and people*, whether I view them as good or bad. This is when my motto, "Everything happens for a reason," comes alive and brings me peace. Everyone, and I mean everyone, has a right to learn their lessons in their own way. Who are we to tell them that they are wrong? If we don't want it in our life, we can change it.

For me, in my marriage and with some of my other relationships, I was sick to death of being told that what I believed was wrong, or inappropriate, or worth getting hit over, for that matter! I had the courage to leave and start over. Why would I want to put that feeling of negative judgment on myself or anyone else when I can remember how awful it felt to experience it? Remember, we are all made of the same energy and I found a whole lot of freedom and peace of mind when I learned to *zip my lip* and practice that old bit of wisdom, "If you don't have something good to say, don't say anything at all."

As I've healed, I have gained confidence in my own opinions about life and don't need others to validate my beliefs anymore. Talk about a sensational feeling! And, if we seek validation or confirmation outside ourselves, going to some close and loving friends or a favorite healer and asking for their opinions in a straightforward, nonconfrontational manner gives us an opportunity to gauge our own confidence by being willing to hear whatever they have to say.

Are You an Animal Lover?

Don't get me wrong here—I do have occasional sadness that comes into my life, but I know how to handle it now and how to not let events pull me down into the dumps like I used to. For example, I received a phone call at 5:20 A.M. from my daughter telling me that their dog, Larry, had died on Christmas morning, and I found myself feeling very sad and down for the rest of the day. I knew that my kids were in a lot of grief and I could almost feel it through the airwaves. But do you know what else I did? I found a way to attempt to make something good come out of it. I let myself have a good cry to release my sadness and then sat down and wrote about it. I sent an email to my friends and family members asking for thoughts and prayers for me and my children, and found myself thinking more about all of the wonderful gifts of joy and happiness that our little friend, Larry, had brought us all of those years. I received such beautiful responses from friends and simply felt better from writing this email. Here it is below:

> Dear friends and family,
> My three children woke up to a very sad loss on this Christmas morning. Their beloved dog, Larry (a part of the family for 12 years), died early this morning during a seizure.
> When we picked him out at the Animal Shelter, we had the

choice of Larry, Moe, and Curly . . . and my son, Bobby, chose our friend Larry. (I never thought that I'd have a dog named "Larry." But, oh and how our good natured, dear "Larry" brought so much joy and happiness into all of our lives.) As any of you animal lovers realize, they become a special member of the family. Bobby even had his graduation picture taken with Larry last year!

My children's father and I often felt like he was our fourth child . . . and we genuinely spoke to each other with compassion this morning, sharing our children's hurt and sadness . . . united as their parents, rather than ex's. That was a welcomed "gift" that our little Larry gave us on this Christmas morning. Death does that . . . it breaks down the walls and defenses, and often brings out the true love that exists among all of us, if we let it.

Please send prayers and extra thoughts of peace and love to my children, Tom, Bob, and Lindsey today. Christmas love is such a giving and joyous love and I just know that if we all join together in sending them a heartfelt healing love on this very special day that *they will feel our warm energy of peace* and blessings.

Just knowing that Larry simply left the physical form—that his spirit lives on in our hearts, our memories, and that he will continue to be around us in our daily lives—gives me a gentle feeling of peace and thankfulness.

This dog was so cherished and brought my children through a lot of pain during our divorce . . . and other life challenges. He gifted them with a true example of unconditional love! And for that I am so grateful!!

Each year as they put up his special "doggy-designed" Christmas tree ornaments (yes, I even bought him ornaments just like I did for the children) that bear his name, they will be able to smile and know that he blessed their lives for many years and that fact will never change or go away.

Thank you and special Holiday blessings to each of you.
With appreciation, love, and peace,

Lori Rekowski

Taking time to write down how you feel, whether in an email to friends or your journal, can always help you process your feelings. This email was a good example of that, with the added benefit of then receiving positive energy from those you can count on in your life for support to help heal the event or situation. And, believe me, the more you heal, the more that list of "supporters" grows in your life.

You see, now that I am much further down the road on my healing path, my focus automatically goes to *finding the good* in every single thing that "happens" in my life, rather than looking through the dark cloud that used to be hanging over my head, robbing me of my passions and joys.

Yes, This Is for Real

If I sound like a coach or cheerleader here, that is exactly what I am intending. As I shared at the beginning of this book, I remember the pain that I went through very clearly. And I do not wish for anyone to go through one single day more than they have to in that old victim mindset or suffer any more of the misery that comes with it.

What I share in this book is by no means "rocket science"; in fact, to the contrary. There are just some very simple steps—plans and actions that you can use to create a happy life for yourself. Sometimes the simplest of ideas are right in front of our faces; we are just too bogged down in fear, self-doubt, and frustration to see them. Get excited about this! This path is the most rewarding one that you'll ever find!

I'm lifting the veil on the clouds of doubt in the coming chapter and am giving you all sorts of techniques that you can use to keep the commitment that you just made to yourself. So here's your first baby step—I encourage you to visit the website www.avictimnomore.com, join a forum, read my blogs, and take a moment to do the interactive breathing meditation, especially when you find yourself feeling overwhelmed.

Please, check in and read how your fellow readers have been able to make changes in their lives by following these insights and exercises. I've kept these exercises and insights short and to the point and very easy to implement. Flip the page and let's dig in and start the process.

13

Insights and Exercises

We are here together, shedding the victim consciousness, one person at a time, beginning with ourselves.

The following is a quick summary of what I have practiced to transcend the victim consciousness in myself. Do not expect perfection of yourself. This is a set of tools. It is all about the process! Focus and stay in the present moment. Act on what you can do right here and right NOW.

You may feel that I put great emphasis on the breathing exercise, but, dear friends, it is one very powerful healing tool! I highly recommend that you practice it throughout your day.

Breathe in your Divinity—receive.
Breathe out your Divinity—give it back.

On your journey to overcoming victimhood and becoming "a victim no more," I suggest that you practice these insights and exercises on a daily basis.

1. Choose to Be Grateful

> The greatest discovery of my generation is that a human being can alter his life by altering his attitude.
> —*William James*

Start your day with an attitude of gratitude, honoring the gift of breath that comes with waking each morning. This will set a pattern for the coming day.

We can all be swept away by negative influences that are around us each day. As I have become increasingly filled with love and light, my sensitivities to the tendencies of others have heightened. Often I will become acutely aware when a friend or family member is focusing on someone else's weaknesses or rude behaviors during a conversation.

When you catch yourself doing this, or find yourself in conversation about something negative or not coming from love and compassion . . . STOP! Stop yourself, stop the conversation, change the subject promptly. Politely end the conversation. This is a great example of learning to honor yourself, and you certainly are honoring the other person, whether they realize it or not. The world has plenty of negative energy out there. As light workers, we are responsible for choosing not to add more to it.

As you practice the "attitude of gratitude," energy will shift around you and you will step back into a place of peace and joy. It may take some practice, but soon choosing to stay in a positive and loving mindset will become effortless. You will experience fewer discomforts that come from negative experiences. If your friends or family members do not respond to you and insist upon continuing negative conversations, you may need to take a break from them for a while. Detach with love. Do whatever it takes to stay in gratitude, for gratitude is the greatest healer of all. It confirms and assures our subconscious self that it is on track and that you are accepting and embracing life, rather than denying the path that you are presently on. One of my favorite little sayings goes like this: "You are what you think about all day long."

Daily Affirmation: "Today, I begin and end my day with gratitude."

2. Focus on Your Desire to Become Godlike

As a man thinketh in his heart so is he.
—William James

God is love. Affirm today to be more love, hold more love, and give more love to others. Know that your God-presence will begin to shine through the clouds under which you have been living. Intend that it will bring forth a powerful sense of peace and joy in your life when you do this. Bring your thoughts right back on an upbeat and positive track whenever you notice you are choosing fear instead of love.

We all have desires we dream of fulfilling. Perhaps it is to be in a new relationship, to be better parents, to have more money, or to travel more often. Whatever it is, desire is our fuel to make those things become a reality. Make it a priority to desire consciously to become more Godlike.

I personally understand "becoming more Godlike" to mean being more loving, tolerant, patient, and peaceful, less willful, and always asking and affirming that the "highest good of all" will occur. But don't limit yourself in your desire. Add, "This or something better is manifesting for me." End the prayer with "and so it is."

We all have a natural, burning desire to feel loved. This desire will not be overshadowed by any experience when we allow ourselves simply to focus our intent on living in our truth. Our truth is what brings us love and happiness.

Daily Affirmation: "I accept more love into my heart today. I freely flow that love out to others, knowing that the source of that love is never-ending."

3. Today, I Am Willing to Forgive Others and Myself

To err is human; to forgive, divine.
—*Alexander Pope*

Forgiveness is the key to finding peace within. Start with yourself. Let's face it, there seems to be a reward somewhere in holding on to a grudge. Those of us who identify with the word "victim" and the pattern of giving our power away to someone or something else can identify with blaming others or outside circumstances for our misfortunes. And, please, there isn't one of us who hasn't had someone betray our confidence or trust in some way. People have broken their word to you. In allowing yourself to be vulnerable (which is unavoidable as a human), you opened yourself to the chance of the pain of rejection, hurt, and disappointment. Many of us became angry, resentful, and most certainly not willing to forgive someone at one point or another in our lives. We even felt justified in holding on to that grudge. The problem is that the feeling of resentment hurt us in the long run and at times didn't even seem to affect the other person involved. We let the resentment simmer and brew and added a bit of blame and shame into that concoction of emotions, which, needless to say, didn't do us any good. We felt angry and miserable about it all.

Now, who really consciously wants to walk around feeling resentment all the time? We are far wiser in the big picture to release our judgments, love unconditionally, and spend our energies on our own healing! Yes, it is easier said than done. But honestly, forgiving yourself frees you from the burden of holding on to anger, which attaches to your own personality. The act of choosing not to forgive someone hurts only you, not the other person. I teach in this book that love is a powerful force of energy. And I think we've all discovered that learning to love *ourselves* is necessary to free us from the pain of victim consciousness.

Martin Luther King Jr. gave us this gem of wisdom: "We must

develop and maintain the capacity to forgive. He who is devoid of the power to forgive is devoid of the power to love."

Give yourself the precious gift of forgiveness today and the burdens that once felt like injustice will melt away. Trust in Divine order, ponder the old adage of "what goes around comes around," study the Eastern beliefs about karma, or do whatever else assists you in the act of forgiveness. There is nothing you have ever done that God cannot or will not forgive. Remember, you are God. Apply your ability to heal yourself through forgiveness.

From 1953 to 1981, a silver-haired woman calling herself only "Peace Pilgrim" (her actual name was Mildred Norman Ryder) walked more than 25,000 miles on a personal pilgrimage for peace. She vowed to *"remain a wanderer until mankind has learned the way of peace, walking until given shelter, and fasting until given food."*

In the course of her 28-year pilgrimage she touched the hearts, minds, and lives of thousands of individuals all across North America. Her message was both simple and profound. It continues to inspire people all over the world.

Below is a beautiful quote from her on forgiveness:

> **I do not even need to forgive people, for I harbor no animosity. If they do evil things I feel compassion for them because I know that they have hurt themselves.**
>
> *—Peace Pilgrim*

I believe that this world could use a lot more compassionate people. I strive to be one of them. I have learned that whenever I place judgment or hold back forgiveness, I am hurting me more than the other person. Why? Because I know that we are all one, a part of each other, all here to learn, grow, and evolve into higher aspects of love.

Daily Affirmation: "*I forgive myself and others today, for the highest good of all.*"

4. Practice Not Judging Yourself or Others Today

> How little do they see what is, who frame their hasty judgments upon that which seems.
> —*Robert Southey*

I subtitled this book "How to Break Free from Self-Judgment" because I found that when I did let go of my need to judge myself negatively (and so incessantly), a whole lot of wonderful things started to shift for me, and I do mean for the better. I became less apt to get down on myself in any way, shape, or form when I let that old pattern go. After all, our feelings of guilt may attract the judgment of others. And who wants that? We get enough of it without drawing in any more! Many of us carry around an unnecessary sense of guilt, shame, and unworthiness. It is time to release those feelings.

I spoke about this insight so many times throughout this book, so, therefore, I will just say a few more things here to recap the importance of breaking loose from that *less than productive* habit.

When we realize that judging others only backfires on us, it becomes sensible to let judgment go and ask your angels or God for assistance in healing it. If happiness and peace are what you truly desire, then letting go of judgment is the key to your freedom. Being discerning is different from using negative judgment. Negative judgment is not based in love; discernment is.

I replaced my old habits of viewing life from the negative "poor me" attitude to one of choosing to look at this world with rose-colored glasses (whether people approve or not). When I say rose-colored glasses, I mean "looking at life through the eyes of love." Rather than constantly talking critically about what isn't working in this world, or who is doing what we perceive as "bad things" (that is being judgmental), I focus on what *is* working. Where your thoughts go, your attention flows, and you have learned enough thus far in this book to know that you do not heal by focusing on the negatives or on the past, but rather on embracing the present moment with gratitude, and blessing all of the gifts that it has to offer. And, of course, we must not forget about focusing on all of the gifts that we have to offer others now, as you move out into the world a much happier and more positive person!

Daily Affirmation: "I release all negative judgments of myself and others today. I accept the gifts of freedom that living without judgment gives me."

5. Apply Humor with Love to Heal Yourself

A keen sense of humor helps us to overlook the unbecoming, understand the unconventional, tolerate the unpleasant, overcome the unexpected, and outlast the unbearable.
— Billy Graham

Humor is a delightful tool to use in releasing victim consciousness. Exaggerating a situation is an especially powerful way to release the pain of that situation. Whether it's fear, impatience, shame, guilt, or frustration that is temporarily holding you back from feeling peaceful and content, a simple exercise is to pretend you are throwing a fit or to lie on the floor kicking and screaming about it. This can bring up laughter and take the power away from the problem.

Attending a comedy, telling a joke, or changing your thought patterns to remember a funny situation from the past can shift your attention away from how you feel in response to an immediate problem and promptly release the resulting negative emotions that are getting you down. Being able to laugh lovingly at oneself is a delightful way to bring light to any situation.

Daily Action: Smile until you are happy. (It works!) Laughter is also a powerful healing tool for discovering your new happiness.

6. Take Responsibility for Yourself

> It is not size or age that separates children from adults. It is responsibility.
>
> —*Jules Feiffer*

Start this process by affirming to apply compassion in all that you do and say. Until I realized that being responsible is simply being "response-able" (or able to respond), I was fearful of owning my responsibility in many situations in which I found myself. I had associated the word "responsibility" with shame-filled and negative experiences from childhood and was thrilled to learn, and grow to understand, that "being responsible" is actually an empowering, healing action to take—and a feeling to own.

Further freedom came when I grew to understand that I had automatically applied negative judgment to myself for difficulties I experienced. Once I released the need to judge myself for my past actions, owning my part in the event or situation became much easier to do. Freedom from judgment makes taking responsibility for your own actions a far easier, love-based task. It brings with it a level of gratitude for the lessons that one has received from the experience.

Daily Affirmation: "I release judgment for my experiences and turn 'taking responsibility' into a grand healing tool! I remind myself that I am 'response-able' in each moment of the day. I celebrate the joy that this freedom brings into my new lifestyle. I am no longer a victim of my past."

7. Be Open and Receptive to All the Joy Life Has to Offer

> If you were all alone in the universe with no one to talk to, no one with whom to share the beauty of the stars, to laugh with, to touch, what would be your purpose in life? It is other life, it is love, that gives your life meaning. This is harmony. We

Insights and Exercises

must discover the joy of each other, the joy of challenge, the joy of growth.

—*Mitsugi Saotome*

Being open and feeling worthy are important conduits for change in your life. And when I talk about being open I am speaking of taking it one step further and suggest that you *step back, widen your perspective, and embrace* every bit of joy that comes your way. Joy is such a beautiful energy. In fact, Reverend Michael Beckwith of Agape International Spiritual Center gave his congregation a wonderful idea in one of his sermons; he encouraged us to take time and pretend that we were visiting with joy, as if it were a friend. Silence yourself and just feel what the energy of joy is really all about. Visit with it, familiarize yourself with it, and have a chat with it. I know that this might sound a bit silly, but why not? As victims, we sure were comfortable with (and knew oh so well) what misery felt like. Why not practice getting to be as comfortable with joy! When shedding the old ways of living in victim consciousness, you must replace the past behaviors and pain with more love, joy, and light to bring fullness and healing full circle. The title of this insight is actually a wonderful affirmation in and of itself and, when set forth *with focused intention*, works wonderfully. That affirmation is an expression of the desire to magnetize all of the wonderful gifts that life has to offer.

Some days when I did not particularly feel like being open and receptive to the goodness that life really has to offer, I would simply state the words "peace, joy, harmony, love, and light" repeatedly. In doing so, I was soon right back into the flow of experiencing positivism.

Daily Affirmation: "*I am open and receptive to all the joy that life has to offer.*"

8. Accept All of Who You Are

> We do not believe in ourselves until someone reveals that deep inside us is valuable, worth listening to, worthy of our trust, sacred to our touch. Once we believe in ourselves we can risk curiosity, wonder, spontaneous delight, or any experience that reveals the human spirit.
> —*e. e. cummings*

We are all made up of negative and positive energy. I'll bet that you accept that without judgment. Some call it darkness and light. It is important for us to accept both the darkness and the light, unconditionally. Do not judge or deny the existence of the darkness. Instead, thank it for the gifts and lessons that experiencing its essence gave you. This is a time when our goal is to transcend and release the darkness and replace it with more light and love.

In this book, I accept that it was the experiences of the dark energies (sometimes manifested in the form of great traumas) that propelled me to seek the light. Owning and understanding that this was actually a gift is indeed an application of acceptance.

Simply admit, "It happened. I did this at the time, for it was all that I understood." Forgive yourself, and then think about what it is that you can learn from the experience. Don't be bashful. Ask your higher self or angels to help guide you to understanding the lesson behind those dark experiences. Listen to the inner voice that is expressing itself through negative experiences and be willing to choose to understand what it is telling you, without judgment.

Your dark side desperately tries to get your attention through episodes or experiences that could be considered negative. These experiences will enlighten you to the reality that "everything happens for a reason," and that through old patterns and experiences, often ones you label "mistakes," you can actually grow to realize that you no longer need to use this type of learning.

Releasing the "right and wrong" judgments frees you to live

in a sense of acceptance and peace. Affirming a knowingness of this truth is a higher way of accepting and transcending your life lessons. Releasing the need to judge your less-than-desirable experiences creates a beautiful acceptance of the Divine order that unfolds as your life.

Daily Affirmation: "*Today I will accept all of who I am. I am willing to own every part of who I am, without judgment.*"

9. Own Your Empowerment

> Believe there is a great power silently working all things for good, behave yourself, and never mind the rest.
> —Beatrix Potter

Some of us have fears about holding power; perhaps, as many believe, from a past-life experience in which we abused our power and still have cellular memory of it, or a time when we were hurt by others who abused their power in this or a previous lifetime.

Choosing not to judge others is actually empowering, because love is all there is. The rest is simply illusion. Learn to say, "I am the creator of that illusion and I can change it." You have the power to act or react in any way you choose, which makes blaming someone else for having given away your power almost impossible.

It is important to understand that once you have chosen the path of enlightenment and released your fears, you begin to change both inwardly and outwardly. You become empowered.

When you begin to own your own power, you start to naturally set boundaries from a place of sincerity, not out of resentment or anger, and those who surround you begin to observe and react to those changes. As I healed and learned to honor myself and own the power that comes with that, my daughter began to do the same. When you heal, those around you also heal. This process might be confusing to others. Understand that when you practice living from your own empowerment, inevitably it does affect those around you. What a gift to give those you love! Whether it becomes obvious right away or in years to come, this process begins to break the pattern of the victim mindset in your family, friends, and colleagues. Now that is a powerful reality!

Daily Affirmation: "I understand that what I do today, the decisions and choices I make in this moment, are what truly create my tomorrows."

10. Give Yourself Some Credit

A man cannot be comfortable without his own approval.
—Mark Twain

"Owning your empowerment" means giving yourself some credit! There is nothing wrong with giving yourself a little recognition for your hard work. In fact, I highly recommend getting used to giving yourself some "kudos." As you come into your own and find your inner peace, you become self-realized and that is a good thing.

I personally give myself credit for being willing to continue my healing process each and every day on this path. For instance, once I was able to start seeking help from a place of *victorhood* rather than victimhood, my desire to understand victim behaviors overall became more important to me. I applied the "burning desire" and "personal power through awareness" insights and felt that if I could understand a little more fully why I had been having such a turbulent roller-coaster-like ride in my life, then I might experience even more of my long-sought-after peace of mind in the process. I was so used to judging myself and being self-critical in the past that I never even took the opportunity to get to understand *why* my behavior patterns were as they had been. As I conducted research for this book, I visited the website for NOVA (National Organization for Victim Assistance). In doing so, I read all about the psychological trauma of crime victimization. It explained the crisis reaction and long-term stress reactions that victims go through. It was a great relief to discover that the roller-coaster ride that I had been on for so many years was actually "normal" or "typical" for someone who had been a victim of violent crimes. I strongly recommend that you go to www.trynova.org and take some time to learn more about the normal reactions and emotions that come with trauma. Once you do, you will feel a greater sense of *compassion for yourself.* As I've mentioned previously, it is important to continue to expand your awareness through the eyes of love and understanding. Give yourself some credit and know that you have the courage within and the inner strength to continue to heal yourself on every level, one step at a time.

Remember, you are a powerful spiritual being who has come to the realization that you can love yourself unconditionally, all of you, and that you are indeed a part of God. You have learned not to judge yourself relentlessly and now know how to set boundaries with others because of that. You celebrate learning and growing each and every day and are free from the shackles of victimhood!

You will soon become "microscopically honest" with yourself and others and, as you do, you will see that by coming from that place of integrity and expressing your authentic feelings, your communication abilities dissolve the misunderstandings that once caused much frustration and uncertainty in your relationships.

You can become the observer, switching your viewpoint to another perspective when you are confused about a situation. Ask your angels to help you with this when you become stuck in a narrow point of view. Ask for assistance in seeing what is for the highest good of yourself and others. The choices that you make from that viewpoint are always more joyful when manifested.

Own and acknowledge the fact that everything is in divine and perfect order, right here and right now, and that you are right where you are supposed to be. This truly is an action of giving yourself credit. And you deserve it!

Daily Affirmation: "I acknowledge all of my hard work and accept credit for the results, with joy."

11. Create Your Divinity

Do not worry if you have built your castles in the air. They are where they should be. Now put the foundations under them.
—*Henry David Thoreau*

We are each unique individuals, full of potential and brilliantly able to learn. With a little persistence and a lot of repetition we can create a life we once only dreamed was possible. We begin to put the foundation down under those dreams.

When mixing your individual desires with love (divinity), you have a sure-fire formula for success in your life. And although we now realize that we are a part of God, we also know that within our uniqueness we all have our own personal identities. The wonderful gift of free will has wreaked havoc in many lives in the past. However, once we become empowered to live from our authentic selves, our true spiritual being-ness, we can begin to create a life that is filled with amazing blessings. When we become aware of our own unique talents and gifts, we can put them to work in service to others and really make a difference in this world.

When applying the "highest good of all" choice to your manifesting process, you begin to have the ability and confidence to create wonderful new experiences, and these new experiences are expressions of your divinity. Take it even further and state, as you create, "For my highest good." You are becoming even more aware that you are indeed a part of the whole, and this awareness changes your life in wonderful ways. You are trusting that "Yes, I am God also." When you create from the place of oneness with God, from your heart center, out of love, you begin to live out your divine purpose. You are living your divinity. You choose positive and loving thoughts and automatically manifest your desires in accordance with divine will. The rewards of a much happier and fulfilling life are rich.

Many of us who have experienced the victim consciousness realize at some point that we have made a mess of our lives, and although on the surface we may have blamed our upbringing, our parents, or other people and circumstances from our past, in the end, we beat ourselves up for our "mistakes" and miserable existence. We also label many of those experiences as unfair, or we simply hold a belief that "life isn't fair." When you begin to take responsibility for your choices, you start to see that beating yourself up for those choices is a waste of time, and forgiving yourself and others is a rocket booster into a new way of thinking and living. The past is the past. Although some of the circumstances and residuals of past choices still need to be resolved and healed on more levels, even the hope, even the thought, of creating a new life can empower you and bring you joy in your daily life. That is what hope is all about—believing in a brighter future and knowing that you can create it.

The fact of the matter is that you can change all of the beliefs that limit you from experiencing joy. You can create a new and exciting reality at any time. I have done it, and so can you! My friends, this is how I created a new reality for myself. Sometimes I simply pretended that I was in a play or movie, acting out my life. I imagined various outcomes and picked the one that felt the best to me. As I kept pretending that everything was fine, a funny thing happened. I actually began to become happy, and I began to manifest more experiences that were pleasant.

Decide to have fun with the creation process and enjoy the power that you have to create a beautiful new life filled with joy, peace, fun, and happiness—a Divine life. Here is the creation process that I use, which you can, too:

- Believe that you can create your dreams, wants, or desires.

- Think thoughts about how you can re-create your life.

- Pretend (feel) that you are already creating happiness and contentment in a particular goal or outcome.

- Detach from the outcome (from exactly how it will all unfold).

You will be surprised at how much better the original desire manifests when you let go of controlling exactly how it manifests. I've found that some of the perceived "side trips" that frustrated me at the time in getting what I wanted turned out to produce something even better than I had originally intended. That is when using the affirmation "This or something better is manifesting for me, and so it is" comes in handy.

A friendly reminder: Early on in our healing paths out of the victim consciousness, we still have a limited view of what it is like to live healthy, spiritual lives on a regular basis. It is important to dig into your tool bag and grab "Know and trust in your divinity" to practice. Your higher self and the angels know what is better for you in the long term. As we move further along on our healing path, we begin to have more joy-filled experiences. Be patient.

We all have a tendency to try to control the "how it's going to happen" part of the manifesting process when we first learn it. Often the tighter we hold on to the way that we think it will unfold—the more it evades us.

Letting go of that control allows the universe to take charge and help us create what is best for us in our lives. In my own personal journey, I've observed something that I had not even thought of, and perhaps you haven't either. There are "others" involved in our lives, and some of those "side trips" I speak of are deliberately arranged so we can cross the paths of people who need our help. Once you start to heal, others are drawn to you, sometimes unknowingly, for lessons, as well. I can see clearly now that I have helped other people by stepping into their lives at just the right time. We are given countless opportunities to guide and counsel each other and, in the process, all of our lives are changed in positive ways.

Remember, we are all part of the Oneness, and we are here to help each other learn and grow. Most of those who cross our paths agreed to do so long before we entered our physical bodies, so we could evolve together. Michael Newton's book *Destiny of Souls* explains this quite clearly. Soon it will become evident to you that you are creating your own Divine place in this world!

Daily Affirmation: "I accept that I can create a new reality for my life."

12. Release Your *Need* to Be Right

> Attachment is the great fabricator of illusions; reality can be attained only by someone who is detached.
> —*Simone Weil*

Once I realized that my *need to be right* was most often fueled by my own feelings of inadequacy and actually was crippling me in many of my relationships and interactions as a whole, I determined that I would be wise to let that habit go. In fact, I realized that I had all kinds of attachments to indoctrinated beliefs in this area. From the years of indoctrination that I had in my religious upbringing to believe that Christianity was the *only way to find god* or to *"be saved,"* I adopted an old pattern that most definitely bled through in other areas of my life. And that old pattern was to consistently engage or be attached to that old "I am right and you are wrong" way of thinking. In fact, we were taught to go and save everyone else and convert him/her to our beliefs. Using force of will is what the Christian Crusades were all based upon in the medieval era. And that way of viewing life inherently caused dramas and uneasiness in my life as a whole.

Frankly, when you need to be right about something, and you

maintain an avid stance on that belief, you have nothing else to resort to but *force of will*.

Once I became aware of my need to be right and how it was fueled by my attachment to certain beliefs, I was able to better understand that if I had a belief that would be so strong that I could not budge from my stance on it, even to the extent that I would actually engage in verbal warfare in order to defend it, well then, I had better be willing to look at that belief and find out where it came from. Love doesn't create arguments, fear does. The fear of being wrong is the culprit. And if I fear that my belief is wrong to the extent that I'll fight for it by forcing someone else to believe it, well then, it probably is an indoctrinated belief that I picked up along the way, not a universal truth that I have found within myself. Truth brings joy. Love doesn't have to be right. Love just loves to love. Love accepts everyone and everything just as they are without judgment.

If we consistently remind ourselves that everything happens for a reason and that everyone is right where they are supposed to be living their own lives in divine order, then what are the grounds to engage in an argument? In fact, we all know that the easiest way to end an argument is by saying to the other person "you're right!" It seems to instantly end the argument, doesn't it? At the very least it gives everyone a timeout to step back, take a deep breath, and rethink the whole conversation. That is a good thing! Stepping back gives us a sense of detachment and gets the emotions out of the way. Diplomacy is all about disengaging from the emotional "hits" caused by our attachments to having the need to be right.

Let me explain further here. Recently, a new friend came into my life. He had a habit of always needing others to see things his way and would get quite irritated when others would resist what he had to tell them. Now, the key words here are "tell them." In fact, he'd become agitated often. He had some fascinating opinions to share, but I soon realized that I became resistant to wanting to listen to any of this information because of the manner in which he was sharing it with me. He had an extreme *need to be right* and when someone has that strong a need, it sets forth the opposite reaction. And that is resistance! Remember that saying from childhood? The one that goes like this: "What we resist, persists!" The funny thing was that although my first reaction was often resistance because of the *manner* in which he was expressing it to me, I later was able to ponder the information and some of it actually made a lot of sense. I then was willing to shift my point of view a bit, and even consider his information as an alternative viewpoint to maintain.

He was a remarkable healer and had a brilliant sense of humor, but no one was coming to see him and he just couldn't understand this. The flags had already gone up for me and I could clearly see why this was happening. I could see that if he actually wanted my help as he said, it was going to take time to get him to see this behavior on his own. Again, this is a clear example of letting someone else come to *his own conclusion* by sharing, rather than by telling.

I often reminded him of the importance of staying out of "the right and wrong game," which, again, we all know can cause a lot of unnecessary problems in our lives. I'd stop him when he'd start rambling on and on about all of the injustices of the world. Funny thing is, I realized that I too had the tendency to need to be right and so I shared with him my own lesson as an example. I love the way the universe has a way of mirroring these kinds of lessons to us.

Now, when we stand this firmly in our particular beliefs, a *push and pull power game* ensues and often turns into a whole lot of negative energy.

None of us needs to gain empowerment through others; we only need to go within for our answers. When we are coming from a space of love, we really don't need anyone else to believe our way; we can just rest in our contentment of living our own personal life of empowerment and seek to make our decisions from "the highest good of all" mindset, trust that it will unfold, and let it go.

I am happy to share that this friend did indeed begin to see his own patterns as I set my own boundaries and lovingly reminded him of his tendencies. Once I let go of my own need to interact with his behavior, he soon found it a waste of time to attempt to persuade me to think his way. He also slowly stopped complaining out loud, as he'd catch himself doing this. It was a joy to see him shift in such a dramatic and delightful manner.

One more point to look at in regard to our *need to be right* is the emotion of shame. Shame puts us into a defensive stance. Our continuous attempt to prove ourselves to others is born out of shame, and its cousins, guilt and blame. We need everyone else's approval because we can't accept ourselves for who we were. Let go of that old shame, blame, and guilt and you will no longer feel the *need* to be right. Believe me, people will be far more apt to *come to you for help* if you simply rest in self-acceptance and acceptance of others, which brings forth contentment. Peace and contentment are rare commodities these days and if you aren't engaged in proving yourself to be right and telling others that they are wrong, well then, they'll want what you have—peace of mind and contentment.

I honor others' rights to live their life in any way that they see fit. I am content being my own personal expression of God-life through acceptance of this present moment and all the gifts that it has to offer. Release that old *need to be right* and you'll find a whole lot more time and freedom to enjoy your friends and the interests that bring you joy.

Daily Affirmation: "I release my need to be right and replace it with acceptance of the fact that all is in divine and perfect order."

13. Let Yourself Feel

> But reason has no power against feeling, and feeling older than history is no light matter.
>
> —*Charlotte Perkins Gilman*

Insights and Exercises

At first, I honestly was afraid to allow myself to feel. I was numb, and I had done just about everything in my power not to feel for most of my life. I binged and purged away my feelings. I worked them away. I drank them away. I kept myself occupied with blaming others, and I projected my misery out at them. I created the dramas to divert myself from having to feel at all!

Eventually, I learned that I held an inner belief that if I let myself really feel the pain and the disgusting hatred I felt for myself, then I would be sucked back into a deep depression and the despair might take me into some big black hole from which I would never be able to escape. A fear of this happening kept me from allowing myself to feel any of my pain. Instead, if I believed that it was a pain that someone else caused, I could cry and moan and scream with rage and get over it, sometimes in as little as a few minutes. The funny thing is, now I have discovered that I can do the same thing with my own feelings, and that it is a natural part of my life.

I began to associate this process with dipping my foot into the water, for just a moment at first, letting myself feel for a moment, and then pulling it back out. I also discovered that when I did not resist the pain, and just sat with it for a bit, it moved through me and away from me far more quickly. And for goodness' sake, I was still okay.

Daily Action: Give yourself an allotted time each day (even if it is just one minute) to sit with, feel, and allow healing of your old "wounds"—and then move right on out of it! When you come from a place of peace within, you have the power and strength, as well as the support from your angels and the Creator, to heal the old wounds, safely and gently. Yes, it may get uncomfortable at times, but it is a time investment that is well worth it.

Daily Affirmation: "Today I will allow myself to sit with any feeling that comes my way. I will observe that feeling, without judgment of any kind."

14. Celebrate Your Divinity

> The more you praise and celebrate your life, the more there is in life to celebrate.
>
> —*Oprah Winfrey*

Celebration is the fun part of this new life that you are living, free from the victim consciousness. Spending time with other like-minded and positive people is a great way to start the process of living a life free from victimhood. You will actually begin to draw people into your life that are more joyful to be around. "Like attracts like," and this universal law is a fun one to experience when living from this happier mindset. Be patient. You will see the changes in your relationships begin, and new and wonderful people will begin to show up in your life. Enjoy!

There are groups forming all over the place that can support you on your healing path. Some gather to watch spiritual cinema movies, some form healing circles, some gather to pray for peace, and others gather to simply play together. There are drumming circles, spiritual book clubs, conscious singles groups, and the list goes on and on. Go celebrate your newfound hunger for enlightenment with hundreds (or thousands in some cases) of other like-minded people. Schedule yourself for a spiritual retreat and meet light workers from around the world. There are a whole lot of light workers just looking for a loving, positive individual to join them, someone just like you. I'd say that is something to celebrate!

Daily Affirmation: "Today, I will reach out and find others to celebrate my divinity with."

15. Give

> Happiness comes when your work and words are of benefit to yourself and others.
>
> —Buddha

This one is simple and to the point. Practice giving to others what you want for yourself. The universe is made of energy. If you give love and support to others unconditionally, they will come back to you in some form or another. Don't expect the person or persons to whom you are giving of yourself, to necessarily be the same people that you get back from. In fact, it's in the element of surprise that people often enjoy the fruits of their labors returning to them. Many spiritual books emphasize the practice of giving what you want for yourself to others because it works! The timeless sayings are true: "What you reap is what you sow"; and "What you put out, you get back."

- Next time you want more prosperity, give a little attention to someone who is struggling in poverty. Be glad for others who have abundance and wish them even more.

- If you are looking for a happy and healthy relationship, say an extra prayer for a special couple in your life so they may have even more joy in their relationship, or encourage a friend to go out on that date he or she has been putting off.

- If you want better health, visit people who are ill. Envision them healthy and bring them some flowers to brighten their day.

I used to tell my daughter that if she wanted to have a better day at elementary school to simply try giving someone a smile when they weren't expecting it. I'd tell her to just smile that beautiful smile of hers at someone that she didn't even know at school—and just see how they reacted. I always reminded her that she was doing it to make someone else's day better, and to just trust that what you put out there comes back in one form or another. She would then give me reports when she would get home. Some days, she'd say that they smiled back at her, and other days, they wouldn't. It was a fun way for her and me to connect as mother and daughter and also a simple way to teach her the importance of giving. Just the very fact that she was willing to give this a try made me a proud mom! I love that many of the schools now have programs during the holidays where they have the kids bring in something to donate for a family in need. They often have canned food donation programs throughout the year as well. Of course, there are many charitable organizations that make a huge difference in the lives of others. There are many philanthropists who have a passion to give back to those who have helped them in times of need. These are all signs to me that our society does indeed encourage us all to be giving to others.

Daily Affirmation: "Today, I will 'pay it forward' and give a simple smile to a stranger on the street."

16. If You Don't Know, Let It Go

> **Good morning. This is God.**
> **I will be handling all of your problems today.**
> **I will not need your help. So, have a good day.**
> <div align="right">—<i>Anonymous</i></div>

Stepping out of the pattern of judging yourself and others, and leaving behind the feeling that you always need to be in control of your environment, creates a new sense of calmness and enlightened awareness. See how delightful it is when you can say, "I choose to let that go." You progressively begin to trust in your intuition, and these responses just become natural.

If a situation arises that feels uncomfortable to me, and my instinctual response is to judge a person or situation, I stop myself and say to myself: "It is that it is," and then let it go. I do not put any more attention or energy into the situation, realizing that my energy is valuable and I no longer intend to waste it on negative responses.

Focus instead on staying in integrity and living joyfully. To do so, you need to stay in the positive flow of love and honor. Of course, you won't always have a clear understanding in the moment of why or how to respond to all of life's circumstances. You don't need to! Your higher self knows exactly what it's doing, even though your mind may not be able to comprehend what's going on in that moment. The answer will come when it's supposed to.

Think about the many times you have tried to force something to happen, when you've been overcome by impatience or frustration, only to let go and have your intended desire manifest at a later time, in a far better way than you could have dreamed of in the first place. It happens when you are far more prepared to enjoy it. Simply surrender to the flow of life. Trust that you are on track at some level. Let your ego go and don't take yourself too seriously. Life is here so we can have fun and be joyous.

I found a wonderful little concept while reading the Tobias materials (www.crimsoncircle.com). Tobias was speaking on just this topic: letting things go. He suggested envisioning your problem or challenge and then imagining that you are placing it in the *oven of grace* for the night. Take it out in the morning, throw it up in the air—and watch it break into tiny little light particles and throw them up to the sky and let them become stars! For some reason that really worked for me. There are all kinds of ways that we can let go and let God. Demanding control over matters that we don't have control over (such as other people) just causes stress on ourselves. I don't know about you, but I've had enough of that to last a lifetime!

When you begin to live from this place of trusting your own intuition, trusting in your connection to God from within, even simple, ordinary tasks will become more joyful and filled with purpose. You need not be a professional healer to heal the world, for you will naturally be enhancing the quality of life of those around you with your new peaceful, confident sense of awareness.

Daily Affirmation: "Just for today, I will take whatever I perceive as a problem, and 'let go and let God.' I trust that all is in divine order. And, so it is."

17. Remember "Integrative" in Your Healing Process

It is only by following your deepest instinct that you can lead a rich life, and if you let your fear of consequences prevent you from following your deepest instinct then your life will be safe, expedient, and thin.
—*Katharine Butler Hathaway*

Once you practice being a victor for a while, you will begin to trust your own instincts. Trust me, it really does happen. You begin feeling more and more confident that you are on solid footing in your own belief systems. Applying the word "integrative" to your healing process is a balanced approach. I mentioned this earlier in the book. All of the years of attending Overeaters Anonymous and Al-anon, not to mention the visits to counselors, psychologists, psychiatrists, and eating-disorder treatment programs, helped me tremendously throughout the years. Of course, I kept missing the important component of finding my own inner connection and faith, and I never quite found the peace of mind until I got more in touch with my spirituality. And, of course, that made all the difference on my own path.

I haven't dismissed the use of traditional therapies at all. Integrative is all about adding and introducing more information from another source. Please do not take an all-or-nothing approach to your healing journey and turn your back on some of those teachers and programs that you've spent time with on the journey to NOW. Everything happens for a reason. And everything and everyone that we've encountered up until now has assisted us in opening up to the new empowerment that we are experiencing.

As I've healed and grown into a happier human being, my spiritual self has guided me back to some of the wisdom I learned from traditional therapies. This goes for psychological and physical well-being overall.

I still had body-image issues from 30 years of being immersed in obsessive behaviors with food. As I progressed on the path to victorhood, I found myself more open to revisiting much of the wisdom and insights that I had garnered from those years of therapy, and I began exploring other alternatives that were available. I ordered a video tape about women who were working on reevaluating their body image, and how the media feeds into eating disorders by showing stick-thin models. I also learned, from reading *The Diet Cure,* that we are not all made to have that same emaciated look that Fifth Avenue advertising agencies tout as the be-all and end-all of feminine beauty. I still pay attention when I get the nudge to revisit a form of healing that I've used in the past.

If you have an eating disorder, go to www.gurze.com and see what types of videos and books they have available. You'll be surprised at how much more open you are to old concepts—ones that you may have once dismissed due to frustration. Put the label of your addiction into the search engines and just see what comes up. I've mentioned many programs and websites throughout this book that have helped me along the way.

I found that humans innately want to help other humans to overcome the trials and struggles that they have been through themselves. I would even venture to say that it is human nature to want to love and help others—once you've stepped out of the habit of judging and opened your mind, body, and soul to taking the highest path possible.

Really, enjoy the opportunity that you have to explore new beliefs and all of the various paths that have led others to their own inner peace.

Daily Affirmation: "I am open to trusting my own instincts and exploring integrative approaches to my healing process. Today, I will pay attention to those inner nudges to go to the next level of peace, joy, and contentment."

18. Be an Emissary of LOVE—Now

Love and kindness are never wasted. They always make a difference. They bless the one who receives them, and they bless you, the giver.
—Barbara De Angelis

We've all heard that "God is love." You may have also heard, "Only love is real, and the rest is an illusion." This whole concept of being an emissary of love makes sense to me more and more every day. In fact, I find a whole lot of joy in flooding my space with love. I often take the time to sit in silence and imagine myself being flooded with love and it is just pouring right back out of me into the area that I live in. I even will choose to flood the city, state, country, and world with the energy of love. I don't need any proof that it is making a difference because I seriously can feel it happening. I see clearly now that it is love that created this world and love that is healing this world. Less pleasant feelings—hatred, greed, and jealousy, for example—were all simply created at a time when love was not present. Hatred, for instance, is a type of ignorance or, as I see it, a lack of the expression of love in the person carrying that emotion. For me, it was important to work hard to accept and release those lower vibrations and feelings and replace them with more love and light. The fun part has been in passing it on! I always ask for more love to pass around, and I can tell you that I've never been turned down. There is always more than enough love to go around.

Insights and Exercises

Ask God and the angels each day to expand your ability to love and be loved. Also ask the angels to fill you with more light so that you might shine even more out into the world. You will be pleased at the results of these requests.

Daily Affirmation: "I choose to be an emissary of love, now. I am a victim no more!"

14

Support Is Available

Love doesn't make the world go round.
Love is what makes the ride worthwhile.
—*Franklin P. Jones*

There is no need to go it alone.

Love is the key to connecting not only to your spirit within, but to the commonality that we share with others. In this chapter, I am sharing out of love the path that I took on my own personal healing journey. Obviously, not everyone chooses the same path, nor would I expect them to do so. As always, I ask you to please simply take what you want and leave the rest.

In my first television interview to promote the first edition of this book, host Tina Johnson of the "Mind, Body, Spirit" show asked for my definition of a "spiritual healing modality." She also asked me to describe various modalities I had used to heal myself. A spiritual healing modality is an art or technique, often an ancient science, which heals body, mind, or soul. It brings to light, into your awareness, the patterns, lessons, and traits you have chosen to experience in this lifetime. Examples include past-life regression, psychic or intuitive readings, astrology, Reiki healing, massage therapy, feng shui, and numerology. Some modalities, such as intuitive readings, assist you in connecting with your higher self or with spiritual guides. They allow you to experience a new perspective of your life, as it is seen from the "other side" or spirit realm. Some modalities help to remove negative implants and negative elementals, repair the etheric body, repair tears and holes in the aura (the energy field around your physical body), and call on the angels and ascended masters to help in this regard.

On my own path, I was led to participate in past-life regression therapy, and the results of the work I did in those sessions had a profound impact on accelerating the healing of my being. I was led to a practitioner by referral from the office of Dr. Brian Weiss (author of *Many Lives, Many Masters*). Years later, I discovered that in her book *Past Lives, Future Healing,* Sylvia Browne shares documented cases of how past-life regression works.

I also discovered that by learning about my numerology and astrology charts, I gained insight into my personality traits, life challenges, and life cycles. Both charts gave me the same information, which confirmed that I was on the right track. I also found great releases, both physical and emotional, by having sessions with massage therapy and Reiki healing. These modalities increase your awareness of many issues, and when you have more awareness, you can gain much momentum on your healing path.

Now that you are aware that these tools are available and have that burning desire to evolve and heal, your higher self and intuition will lead you to just the right modality. You can start by visiting your local metaphysical store. I believe it is important to share some insights and experiences with you about these stores. There are hundreds if not thousands of metaphysical stores in the United States and several that I found early on in my search for healing proved to be invaluable resources.

I still chuckle when I share this story with people. It was my first visit to a metaphysical store. I was led to one of the most established stores in Minneapolis, Minnesota. As soon as I opened the door and stepped inside Present Moment, a retail business more than two decades old, I practically put up a cross with my fingers! The old Baptist teachings—phrases like "of the devil" and other fear-based admonitions about not looking outside the Bible and Christianity—came flooding into my consciousness the moment I set foot in the store. I cannot tell you how fast those fleeting thoughts left me, however, when I started to look around. A sense of peaceful knowingness came over me as I scanned the books, cards, music recordings, videos, herbal remedies, and gift items. That sense of peace came from within and washed over me. There really were no words that anyone could have said to me in that moment that could have changed my mind about being there. I felt like I was at home. It was similar to that feeling of love sent to me by the robed beings the night of my near-death experience. It was a very strong and almost urgent sense of trusting in my inner being, that I was right where I was supposed to be. That feeling propelled me to explore what the store could offer me.

I felt like a kid in a candy shop. Almost immediately, I noticed there were books arranged by topic and religion on the shelves. That, in and of itself, spoke of "choices and options" to me—something I had longed to find, a way to discover my own truth. I just naturally allowed my intuition to guide me to the right books and information, and what a wonderful feeling that was! Each of us is drawn to the right materials at the right time, and each of us has a unique way of creating that path. Some of us are drawn to Native American teachings, while others are attracted to spiritual traditions from the East. Still others are fascinated by those who can communicate with people who have passed away, or with guides from "the other side." Some browsers are even led to topics they never anticipated, something they suddenly resonate with in the moment, such as finding abundance, finding a "soul mate," or mental or physical healing modalities.

I had an almost ravenous hunger to learn more, and I soon found myself drawn to another experience. A woman at my doctor's office just happened to give me the business card of a woman who had given her an intuitive reading. I put the card in my wallet that day. Months later, I was guided to drive out of the Twin Cities to the busy main street of Stillwater, Minnesota. I discovered the Shoppe of Enlightenment and walked in. I slowly looked around the store, at books, at gifts, and then I inquired whether a reader was available. I decided it was time to have my first intuitive reading. A few minutes later, I was sitting in front of a reader. I looked over at her business card fastened on the wall next to me and, much to my surprise, I recognized the business card as the same one I had tucked away in my wallet months earlier. With that, my nerves calmed. I knew that this was a confirmation for me that I was at the right place, at the right time.

Many times in the years that followed, I also frequented Metaphysical Emporium, a full-service shop that relocated from White Bear Lake to Oakdale, Minnesota. I found that the owners and employees of all three of the stores I've mentioned were very special people. I felt a strange recognition with some of the employees and sensed that I "knew these people before." There was a sense of familiarity with them that I couldn't explain. Each time I was drawn to visit a store, it felt a bit like I was "going home" and that I was about to have a "divine appointment" with someone or some experience. How grateful I am to have found these stores.

I have a lot of respect for the people who had the courage to open the first metaphysical stores. I know many of them were ridiculed and even received hate letters and threats from local religious groups and community members. Some of these shop owners never had a bit of retail experience but were "told" (given visions or nudges) to open their stores. It is important to patronize metaphysical stores, as they are truly serving us in a way that is much needed in this world.

Most stores have information boards where local healers and practitioners display their business cards and announcements of classes and seminars. Many of these store owners and employees are more than willing to answer any question and guide, assist, and educate you on the vast amount of information readily available to help you on your healing path.

Partly due to the courage of these store owners, we've all benefited from an increased presence of healing and metaphysical ideas in the media, including mainstream magazines focusing on feng shui, yoga, aromatherapy, waterfall relaxation, massage, herbal remedies, and much more. A growing number of national and regional talk show hosts are exploring psychic phenomena, "intuitive" development, miracles, angel and ghost sightings, past lives, and many more topics regarding enlightenment and self-awareness.

Again, I encourage you to visit metaphysical stores so that they can continue to offer their personal experiences, insights, wisdom, products, referrals, and services for years to come. It surely has made a difference in my life!

Also be aware that there are some amazing churches and spiritual communities that offer inspiring, open-minded services. The Unity and Spiritualist churches were two of the first organizations to introduce this higher path of learning. There are many other organized groups you can join on your new journey as well. Check the bulletin board at a metaphysical store or in alternative, metaphysical, and wellness magazines that are often found in local coffee shops and neighborhood food co-ops, and you'll find advertisements for all kinds of gatherings of like-minded people.

I wish blessings upon each of you on your path. I celebrate your choice to join us in bringing heaven here to our precious planet. Welcome home! The God within me honors the God within you!

Recommended Reading and Resources

Books That Made a Difference in My Life

Bach, Richard. *Jonathan Livingston Seagull.* New York: Macmillan, 1970.

———. *Illusions: The Adventures of a Reluctant Messiah.* New York: Delacorte, 1977.

Chopra, Deepak. *The Seven Spiritual Laws of Success: A Practical Guide to the Fulfillment of Your Dreams.* San Rafael, Calif.: Amber-Allen/New World Library, 1994.

Dyer, Wayne. *Pulling Your Own Strings.* New York: T. Y. Crowell, 1978.

Ford, Debbie. *The Dark Side of the Light Chasers: Reclaiming Your Power, Creativity, Brilliance, and Dreams.* New York: Riverhead, 1998.

Grabhorn, Lynn. *Excuse Me, Your Life Is Waiting: The Astonishing Power of Feelings.* Charlottesville, Va.: Hampton Roads, 2000.

Hay, Louise. *You Can Heal Your Life.* Santa Monica, Calif.: Hay House, 1987.

Newton, Michael. *Journey of Souls: Case Studies of Life between Lives.* St. Paul, Minn.: Llewellyn, 1994.

———. *Destiny of Souls: New Case Studies of Life between Lives.* St. Paul, Minn.: Llewellyn, 2000.

Redfield, James. *The Celestine Prophecy: An Adventure.* New York: Warner Books, 1993.

Roman, Sanaya. *Personal Power through Awareness: A Guidebook for Sensitive People.* Tiburon, Calif.: H. J. Kramer, 1986.

Ruiz, Miguel. *The Four Agreements: A Practical Guide to Personal Freedom.* San Rafael, Calif.: Amber-Allen/Publishers Group West, 1997.

Sutphen, Richard, and Tara Sutphen. *Soul Agreements.* Charlottesville, Va.: Hampton Roads, 2005.

Virtue, Doreen. *Healing with the Angels: How the Angels Can Assist You in Every Area of Your Life.* Carlsbad, Calif.: Hay House, 1999.

———. *Divine Prescriptions: Using Your Sixth Sense—Spiritual Solutions for You and Your Loved Ones.* Los Angeles, Calif.: Renaissance Books/St. Martin's Press, 2000.

Walsch, Neale Donald. *Conversations with God: An Uncommon Dialogue.* New York: G. P. Putnam's Sons, 1996.

My Favorite Websites

The Tobias Channelings by Geoffrey Hoppe
www.crimsoncircle.com
The Crimson Circle was started in 1999 by a group of Colorado-area light workers. The Crimson Circle gatherings are open to all who are on the spiritual journey.

www.weshamilton.com
Wes Hamilton is a master numerologist who has helped hundreds of people on their healing journey, including me!

www.positivepause.com/en/index.html
This site offers a beautiful animated reminder of who we are and what it's all about.

www.oriahmountaindreamer.com
"The Invitation" is one of my all-time favorite poems, and you'll enjoy the wisdom that you'll be gifted with from this site.

www.orindaben.com
The official website of Orin, DaBen, Sanaya Roman, and Duane Packer. I've read the entire series of books by these authors and I enjoy on a regular basis "creating your highest future room" for daily inspiration and insight at this site.

www.1spirit.com
This is an international spiritual directory of people, places, products, and services dedicated to assisting those on a spiritual path.

Star's Edge International/Avatar
www.avatarEPC.com
I went through this course early on in my healing journey and enjoyed an incredible amount of healing as a result.

www.cardsbycarolyn.com
Another resource for spiritual greeting cards, business cards, and other fun stuff!

Andreas Moritz
www.ener-chi.com
Andreas is an amazing healer and author. Your state of health, vitality, and happiness largely depends on the balance between your body, mind, and spirit. The Ener-Chi Wellness Center is a source of practical and powerful information.

Music That Heals

Enya—A Day without Rain is one of my favorite compact discs.

Healing Waters, by Dean Evenson (www.peacethroughmusic.com)

> **Sometimes, on the way to a dream...**
> **...You get lost and find a better one.**

There are many more wonderful books, music, and websites that led to my awakening and healing. Ask for guidance when you walk into your favorite spiritual gift store or bookstore, and trust that you will be led to the appropriate information for that moment. The materials will indeed "jump out at you." Be sure to pay attention to recommendations from friends and family—and strangers, as well. There are no coincidences. You are right where you are supposed to be, and all truly is in divine order.

Everything happens for a reason, just believe.

About the Authors

Lori Rekowski, a mother of three, has been a business entrepreneur and consultant for more than 25 years. She takes great pride in celebrating her healing process with others. In fact, she considers it her life purpose and passion.

A creative and analytical approach to her healing path during the past twenty years included research and participation in the holistic healing field. After years of seeking help from the traditional psychological health field, Lori was unsuccessful at maintaining long-term emotional stability. She knew (had faith) that there had to be a more effective way to emotional and spiritual stability. Lori found that the most effective assistance, allowing her own healing to accelerate, was the research and application of ancient healing modalities that are resurfacing in our society today, integrated with traditional medicine. Lori studied hundreds of books, experienced private healing sessions, and attended various seminars and classes throughout the United States, internationally, and on the Internet. She focused attention on her own unique inner connection to God and used the spiritual self-help field to heal successfully. This approach, and use of these tools, accelerated her healing process at an amazing pace. She works hard at teaching these tools to other survivors, assisting them in stepping into a healthy and happy lifestyle. You can follow her Facebook Page at https://www.facebook.com/pages/A-Victim-No-More to stay motivated to become free from the victim mindset.

Tim Miejan is a 27-year veteran of print media. A graduate of Missouri Western State College, he served for 12 years as a reporter and editor for the *St. Joseph News-Press*, St. Joseph, Missouri, a daily newspaper serving Northwest Missouri. In 1995, he moved to the Twin Cities of Minneapolis and St. Paul, Minnesota, and became managing editor of the *EDGE*, a free monthly periodical promoting personal growth, integrative healing, and global transformation. In 2004, he coordinated the redesign of that publication and the creation of *Edge Life* magazine, which focuses on holistic life, integrating spirit into daily activity and progressive perspectives on politics, the environment, relationships, and community. He is now a co-owner of this magazine. His interviews of notable leaders in consciousness and healing have been reprinted by online publications in Germany and Italy, and in print magazines *Advaita Journal* (Germany) and *Stoppinder: A Gurdjieff Journal for Our Time*.

.

Notes

Notes

Congratulations! After reading *A Victim No More! How to Break Free from Self Judgment,* your passion is on edge to take life in your own hands!

And you're thinking, "Do I have to do this alone?"

Absolutely not—you're not alone! Finally, the first and only simple, hands-on, interactive, life-transforming on-line experiential course designed with you in mind. Continue your journey to greater understanding with principles that anyone, anywhere can apply. It takes you by your hand, step-by-step on your personal journey to *building your self-worth*. And for the first time, a guide that helps you truly *let yourself be loved! You're worth it!*

You'll have fun as you work through these 18 powerful insights. Just one of these mental training exercises will surprise you by how effective it is. Here's a tiny taste of what you'll find on-line:

- Beautifully framed messages for printing and posting.
- One-of-a-kind flash movies that reaffirm the principles of the materials.
- Fun, easy-to-use and totally interactive course.
- Be continuously reminded that your journey from victimhood to independence is real!
- You could find yourself less stressed, more encouraged, and more motivated!
- Provides you ample opportunity for creative expression.

And you're not alone! Enjoy direction through a special on-line forum with others just like you, healing their way out of victimhood!

And lots more!

Here is how you can change your life in a heartbeat:
Visit: www.avictimnomorecourse.com,
send an e-mail to: order@avictimnomorecourse.com,
or mail a self-addressed, stamped envelope to:
Ron J. Oberon & Associates
150 S. Glenoaks Blvd. # 9342
Burbank, CA 91502

Printed in Great Britain
by Amazon